Beyond NDEs

Beyond NDEs

The Next Step in
Near-Death Experience
Research

By

Lynn K. Russell

Ivey Enterprises
Lethbridge, Alberta, Canada

Beyond Near-Death Experiences
by Lynn K. Russell
Includes bibliographical references

Editor's note
The details and circumstances are as reported. Names of individuals may be changed or omitted to protect the privacy of those mentioned in this publication.

ISBN
paperback: 978-1-7382808-0-3
    e-Book: 978-1-7382808-1-0

Contact Lynn Kathleen Russell through her website:

lynnkrussell.com

This book is dedicated to all the magnificent people who willingly shared their story so that the rest of us could discover and grow in love

Acknowledgements

I want to thank Jill Ebsworth and Jean Peiffer; you offered caring support, editing, and valuable critiques. Jeff Long MD, thank you for the opportunity to research with you and your wife, Jody Long, J D. During this process, I had the chance to study the beautiful messages brought back. In addition, you willingly offered your ongoing support and interest. Thank you. Thanks to Barb Cook for your comments, assistance, and ideas and to Carol Malinauskas for your suggestions, thoughts, and encouragement. Karen Stankunas, thank you for your magic in putting this book together. Shirley Wilson and your wonderful patience, this book would never have gotten this far without you.

Table of Contents

Prologue

A Spiritual Experience

The world of spirituality was, for me, a confusing disarray to slosh around in my search for truth. It seems I was born with an overactive curiosity gene, so many directions presenting themselves for my investigation. As strange as it may seem although my home that knew no religion, my greatest interest has been, and is, spirituality.

Fortunately, our non-religious home offered no preconceived ideas of the truth, and I was completely free to explore to my heart's content. No one told me what not to think, and no restricting ideas of how the world should look were pushed in my direction. As each philosophy came my way, I freely picked it up, turned it this way and that, rattled it a bit, and finally unwrapped it to find out what was inside. I dug down to each religion's origin and scrutinized its various components it encompassed until my unbridled curiosity was satisfied and became free to move on in another direction.

Being raised in a Judeo-Christian country, I naturally explored those disciplines first and discovered the foundations of the faiths my world had been built upon. Once I understood the history and development of these religions and how they had evolved as they had, I carefully put them away and investigated the Christian offshoots: Jehovah's Witnesses, the

Church of Latter-Day Saints, the Salvation Army, and Fundamentalist Baptist, to name a few.

At the time, I tried bumping my head against Eastern philosophies, but my teen self could not imagine a world where personal possessions were not important. Let's face it: I was the normal Western teenager and, quite frankly, thought those guys were nuts. Interestingly, years later, I returned to those beliefs and can now see the beauty and depth of the Zen Buddhist path.

Was I just curious, or was I searching for somewhere I could feel at home? It didn't seem to matter, and over the years, I found many fascinating concepts within each expression of the spiritual as that deep place within drove me onward to find answers. *Why do I exist? How does life happen? Is there a higher power? If so, what role does he/she/it play in our lives?*

By 1973, I was a single parent to our three small children, ages 2, 3, and 4. I had returned to school in the hopes of eventually getting a decent job and providing a better home for us. It was spring, and I had finished my second year at college and was looking forward to summer's promise of hot sun and a time to relax before returning to another year of study. That's when I received a gift that took me by the hand and led me toward the deeper spiritual understanding I sought.

It was a quiet time at our house as Leah, my oldest daughter, was now in grade one, Brad, the middle child, attended afternoon kindergarten, and Wendy, the youngest, was tucked away for an afternoon nap.

When this new adventure began, my hands were stuck in hot, sudsy water as I mechanically washed the lunch dishes. Abruptly, it was as if a mysterious force took over my mind, and I lost complete awareness of where I was and what I was doing. From the window above the sink, the crabapple tree in the backyard seemed to stretch out to me. Oddly, the tree seemed to have me in an embrace that revealed a bizarre new reality.

Understanding beyond reason overwhelmed me, and I knew, deep in my core, that the tree out there and I were one. We were inseparable. Without warning, in a flash, in a way I could not comprehend, I indisputably knew the tree and I had become indivisible; we were a single being.

As I flowed along on this current of experience, a bottomless pool of knowledge surrounded me. I somehow knew deep in my gut the essence within the tree was the same spirit as was in me. We shared a mysterious, inexplicable bond.

Delight and understanding rushed through me, and I was filled with wonder. Within that happiness, a contented feeling told me everything was in its proper place, and all was as it should be.

Unaware of the suds dripping on the floor from my hands, I stood mesmerized while other forms of life went through my mind. Fish and whales in the ocean, lions, and elephants in the wild—shared that same life. I truly became the bird sitting in the tree, and simultaneously, I was the bug the bird was about to eat. We were one single entity expressing itself as life on this planet. Each life's form was irrelevant as I became entirely enmeshed with the essence of that Oneness. In that state, it was impossible to define where the other forms of life ended, and I began because there were no differences, no separations.

Then, within a microsecond, I became aware of the physical world around me and water dripping on the floor.

This awareness happened before most of North America knew the term *Oneness*. It was a time when baby boomers were engrossed in seeking a new spirituality. Many had turned away from the formal churches and were exploring the meaning of life. The Beatles visited ashrams, and Friedrich Nietzsche's claim "God is dead" became a familiar chant.

It is difficult to say how long I was caught in that alternate reality, perhaps a minute, possibly less. Not surprisingly, the effects of that experience offered me a lifetime of learning. Up to that moment, I had sought understanding through established faiths. Now, another route to spiritual answers opened to me. I knew the world was not a bunch of separate beings busily living life. I understood that deep in the core of us all, an amazing connection waits to be recognized. The fact I didn't yet understand what had happened was not a problem and gave me fodder to chew on in my quest for the truth.

As it turned out, the experience while washing the dishes was to be the first of a series of parallel events. A few days later, during another quiet afternoon, I busily spot-washed fingerprints from the hall walls. The quiet house had lulled me into peaceful contemplation of nothing in particular. Without warning, in a flash, once more my awareness was overtaken by a powerful force.

Seconds before I had been washing marks off the walls, suddenly, I was intensely immersed in the awareness of an atom. I allowed them to float in this curious direction without trying to capture my thoughts and return them to where they had been. I allowed them to float in this curious direction. Before me was an atom with its nucleus and electrons spinning around the core. It was as though each element possessed an independent consciousness and knew exactly what it needed to do and got busy doing it. The planning and order within the atom dominated my awareness.

Once recognition of what I was shown entered my consciousness, the image transformed as though I were seeing a new scene in a movie. I was looking at a representation of our solar system whirling in the darkness of space. The sun contentedly sat in a semi-stationary position while the planets busily spun around it in a perpetual game of tag. I became aware of the deliberate order, rhythm, and intelligence behind what I was viewing.

Let me clarify; it was not like an external brain was operating our solar system, like a wizard with a wand. It was that this mental capacity had permeated within the solar system itself. Inexplicably, deep within was a part of me that realized I already knew this and was simply being remind What I saw was not the result of a lucky accident.

Once more, the scene expanded from our local solar system to the Milky Way galaxy as it spun in a golden pirouette along with sister galaxies that whirled together in an amazing pattern of synchronicity. Again, I knew that none of this was an error. Nothing, not a single thing, had mistakenly come to be. There was order and planning in the operation of the universe.

As I delighted in this new understanding, a realization overtook me that kept me reeling in wonder for many years. No voice spoke, yet the knowledge swept through me and became implanted in every cell of my body. The message was so powerful I was immobilized to dispute or deny its meaning.

"Your being is intricately connected with the operation of the universe!" it told me.

I couldn't deny the truth of what I had just learned. It was as real as the Earth I stood on, as real as my children or my own name. Yet, a part of me instantly wanted to reject the message. I became caught in a struggle where disagreement was not possible. The message rang too true to debate, but the implications behind the statement scared me.

Confusion dominated as the experience faded, leaving me clutching a wet rag in the hall. *But,* I argued, *I don't have delusions of grandeur.* I was completely convinced that when it came to the universe, I was smaller than a speck of dust, smaller even than a photon. So, how could my being have anything to do with the operation of the universe?

If this information had come to me in a dream or as one of my thoughts, I would have been free to dismiss it. Yet, the manner in which it came seemed to deny me that option. Indeed, the realization of the truth of what I was told scared me most. If I accepted this universal connection, what would be expected of me? Would I be responsible for doing something I was sure to mess up? Until recently, I had lived life as a mentally slow person and only recently discovered I did not belong to that assessment. Still, the experience and accompanying information came from a source beyond disagreement.

A few more days passed before I had the third and last of these strange events. In contrast to the confusion and fear of the previous communication, this final experience brought great serenity, joy, and deeper understanding.

Understanding what was happening eluded me, an unknown force led me into a world of mystery and incredible joy. I stood in the living room on a quiet afternoon, my hands filled with retrieved toys. I became acutely aware I was not alone. I could feel a palpable, literal presence in the room with me. My eyes saw nothing more than the room and furnishings, yet I knew deep in my gut there was "someone" there. I hesitate to call the presence sharing the room a being or person because no being I knew could cause what happened next.

I felt engulfed in an enormous blanket of love, peace, and joy that was beamed at and into me from every direction by this mysterious force. It felt so good I allowed the experience to wash over me hoping it would last forever.

Then, as though an umbilical cord in the center of my being directly connected me to the invisible presence. Somehow, the positive energy force and I were intricately linked in a way I did not understand. Happily, I basked in the pleasure of the never-ending love and peace. And it was then I heard actual words.

Unlike the information I had received earlier, impressions and thoughts poured into the center of my being. The words were clear and as open as a sweet child's face. They were spoken directly into my right ear with unmistakable clarity: "This is where you came from, and this is where you will return."

Then, as ripples in water calm to nothing, the experience was over, and I stood alone in the room with no presence, no voices, and no blanket of love and joy. Yet the feelings that remained kept me in a state of bliss for months. I could have walked through a meat grinder and come out smiling at the other end. Nothing bothered me. The children's high-pitched noises usually set my nerves on edge. Not during those months. They could make silly noises all they wanted. I existed in a world of pure serenity.

Before this final experience, I had been terrified of dying. My atheist mom believed that once a person died, they disappeared. There was no confusion or theology to confound the situation. We were nothing more than biological beings, and when that gave out, so did we.

That was what terrified me. I didn't want to vanish into nothingness. I wanted meaning and purpose, and the idea of being nothing more than a piece of quivering biology sent a shudder down my spine. With the last of these amazing and mysterious experiences, a new bit fit into I may not have fully understood how it worked, but I knew with complete certainty that I would continue to exist when I died. A secondary change happened after my spiritual experiences. All my life, I had been a serious nail-biter. I gnawed them back so far that my teeth couldn't grasp what was left. When I ran out of nails, I moved on to chewing the skin around the nails. They were ugly and often bleeding.

After these beautiful experiences, one day, I looked down at my hands and realized I had nails. Without being aware of it, I had stopped biting them. It seemed to happen on its own.

It took many years for me to put these spiritual events together and make coherent sense of them. Gradually, a picture of our Oneness became clear, and I began to understand a new reality. Books on spirituality began to make sense. Two that stood out and guided me were *A Course in Miracles,*[1] which talked about forgiveness, letting go of the ego, and seeing ourselves as beautiful beings. Joel Goldsmith's *Parenthesis in Eternity*[2] talked about our connectedness with all that exists. Since then, additional studies have verified and strengthened what I learned from my personal experience.

1

Messages From Beyond

As far back as humans first wondered at the rising of the sun that filled them with warmth and life, we have been driven to realize the answers to our deepest questions. In our quest to know throughout history and until today, we have pulled apart everything in our path to learn how it does what it does. We are driven by an insatiable longing to discover the secrets of the universe and the role, if any, it has for us, or we have within it. Our search has instigated us to tinker in one direction. If we realize we are heading the wrong way, we drop what we are doing and eagerly dash off on another path. Our searches have led to the construction of giant pyramids, powerful organizations, and numerous holy places scattered throughout the world. Yet our questions continue to stream into the cosmos in our insatiable craving for answers.

While we humans love a mystery and to dig our fingers deep into the unknown to find the secrets within, once an enigma's underbelly is revealed, and no mystery is left, there is a feeling of let-down. We convince ourselves there must be more and wonder what we have missed. Then we poke it, turn it over, and tear the unknown apart until we come to understand. In the process of our search for spiritual knowledge, many philosophies have evolved that offer their comprehension of order and stability to reduce our confusion about the universe, our place in it, and the meaning of life and death.

Paleoanthropologists, in an effort to discover how it all began, unearthed a Neanderthal burial site that dated back one hundred thousand years and were amazed to find the first indication early humans considered the possibility of an existence beyond this life.[3] Deep in a cave, the body of a boy was buried with the head of a deer to take with him on his journey. This burial site illustrates, even then, the human struggle for answers to some of our deepest questions stretching back to when we were rubbing sticks together to create fire.

Resolutions to the ongoing mystery of our demise have been a complicated labyrinth, twisted by numerous factors. Like a tall person shoving in front of a child to see a parade, these factors have been thrust in our way and blocked our getting to the truth we seek. Our fears, personal views, religious teachings, cultures, and demands for proof have become hurdles in finding answers to our spiritual questions. And, as curious creatures, it's not good enough to know we live on—we want to know how, where, and what we will do there? We want it all.

Shamans, philosophers, and spiritual leaders have offered their wisdom and sought to tone down our fears and make everything right by telling us what we want to know. Many faiths evolved to take on this task and teach us how to live to ensure a good death. Yet these same leaders were instructed by the same thoughts and ideas passed down from their ancestors. Thus, their answers were not much better than those of the people before them.

Amazing luminary teachers throughout history have offered remarkable insights and sound judgments. But, by the time it filtered down to us, it became like gossip whispered in the ear and passed along until the last person heard a completely different message than the original. The value became confused, misinterpreted, and lost its initial meaning.

Is the wall of mystery that has stood in our way finally crumbling? Are we, at last, getting answers to our age-old questions from those who have been there? Are those who have returned from a near-death experience able to provide us with a new way of seeing? Is a direct link to our answers being offered?

Two major points need to be stressed. My role in these experiences is as a reporter. I do not manipulate the information to fit my outlook or desires because I have none. In doing the research, I was as much a learner as the individuals having the experience. The thoughts and information come from the numerous NDErs sharing their experiences, not from me.

Also, this book does not intend to start a new religion or cult. Although we may have some questions answered, new ones pop up as quickly as Kleenex from a box and may take us in a whole new direction. Therefore, I hope that answers will be found in this book, be aware this is just one more step along the continuum of our spiritual development.

It was a pleasure to do research with Dr. Jeffrey Long, MD, and his wife, Jody Long, JD, the owners of the site Near-Death Experience Research Foundation (NDERF). The research was for a book that Dr. Long has since written, *Evidence of the Afterlife*: *The Science of Near-Death Experiences,* which talks about the scientific investigation into the authenticity of the near-death experience.

During this research, I became like a child at Christmas, hungry for more and more as I tore off the shiny wrapping and searched each account to discover the gift inside. Every report was dissected and reassembled into separate elements of that individual's experience. With enthusiasm, I consumed the stories of the NDEs in large gulps. By the time I had ingested a few hundred reports, I began to see a pattern. *Wait a minute, I told myself, something is going on here.* It seemed that within these people's experiences were deeper messages like buried treasures brought back from beyond the curtain of death. Each crumb coalesced into an observable and definite understanding, and tantalizing secrets started peeking through.

When the research was finished, I couldn't stop learning from people's experiences. I continued to gobble down around 2,500 reports while my fascination turned to a deeper understanding of these secret messages. A hidden legacy being brought back as a marvelous inheritance that was ours all along. It is the hope of this book to pass this heritage on to you.

In 1975, Dr. Raymond Moody published a book that shocked and intrigued everyone. Many rushed out to buy a copy of *Life After Life.*[4] Dr. Moody courageously presented the first book to reveal what people who had been resuscitated after dying talked about their experience. Over time, repetitious information they disclosed prompted further questions. If these people had been dead, how could they know what had happened during their operations or the details of attempts to resuscitate them? His book became so popular that a flood of people wrote about their personal experiences and added to the understanding. I, too, joined the throng as my inquisitiveness sought answers to the mystery of death. Now, no matter how many near-death experiences I have enjoyed reading, I continue to seek out new ones and never tire of them.

Continuing education continues beyond the completion of our time in this physical existence. Those who returned from an NDE explained that the knowledge they gained was not so much a continuation of their education as it was a remembering of things they had already known. So much of the knowledge from the NDEs carefully wrapped in their memories involved information they felt the world urgently needed to understand.

Throughout this book are amazing pieces of knowledge and hopefully answers to the constant questions that will not disappear. Does this knowledge mean we have all the answers? Clearly no. However, many of the religious restrictions of the past have been peeled away, and we are free to explore and discover. We consider the multiple discoveries science makes daily we realize the doors to understanding have barely cracked open. There are many journeys beyond those gates to take us to places only our imaginations can create.

I want to sincerely thank each one who shared their experience with us. Their contributions to our learning have been invaluable and provided an opportunity for deeper understanding we have searched for throughout the centuries. At the last count, there are over four thousand reports on NDERF and counting.

One upsetting trend in the field of NDE research is twisting itself around the subject and weakening its reality. While writing this book, I went to YouTube to watch some NDEs and was both disappointed and astonished to see what had happened with the subject since my last visit. There were links to Ouija boards, crystal gazing, and fundamentalist religious groups vying to take over the focus. While it's not my place to disqualify anyone's experience, there are some important points to consider.

No two people have the exact same experience, no matter how close they may seem. An atheist may see Jesus and become a Christian, a Christian may experience something similar to the Buddhist tradition, and a Jew may experience something very different from what they thought. Each individual has the near-death experience that's right for that specific person. Therefore, no one who has had an NDE can talk with authority about what happened to others who also had an NDE.

It is important to talk about the number of reports of children who died from drowning. Based on the information received at NDERF, the major cause of accidental death with children is drowning. It was the highest on the list by far.

Within this book, subjects that could be sensitive to some people, such as suicide or hellish experiences, have been reported anonymously. However, there are a couple of people who requested I offer links to their sites or stories. Therefore, that information is included in the notes at the back of the book. In an effort to be respectful and sensitive to those who have offered their story, I have been careful not to alter their material except for grammar and brevity. Most of the testimonies mentioned have come from NDERF and researcher Kevin Williams's website, near-death.com. I encourage you to visit these sites and wish you an enjoyable journey in your explorations.

2

The Light

Imagine a world covered with thick and dense clouds day after day. The world is shadowed as dark and murky as the depths of a Stephen King novel. If this were a reality, the imagination would be a moot point because, without light, we would line up to eagerly follow the dinosaurs and cease to exist. The sun's light is essential to our survival. It brings warmth and food and keeps us from shriveling into nothingness in the perpetual darkness.

Yet we are told of a different kind of light more essential to our existence than our sun. It is utterly beyond human ability to conceive, although those who have been with this Light return in a state of awed ecstasy and tell of a Light-Being that far exceeds the brightness of the Big Bang. Although near-death experiences vary, accounts of the Light present very little disparity, as if those NDErs who had this experience had watched the same movie.

Entangled within the brilliant Light is a Being filled with more love than anyone knew was possible, as if every molecule of the universe was awash in love. And, in fact, it is!

While NDE accounts of the Light vary little, the methods of getting there are as diverse as the world's transportation systems. Some folks felt they became like astronauts traveling at warp speed through a wormhole. Others wondered if they had been expected as they were blanketed by the Light, the moment they left their bodies. Some found themselves drifting in a black void, staring at a pinprick of light far in the distance that came closer and closer until they were completely engulfed in light.

Although they may have had little trouble explaining their journey toward the Light, without exception, attempts at explaining the Light itself met with frustration. People stumbled over the details as though they were in an extremely strange land and did not know the language. The most common portrayal was of looking at the brightness of a thousand suns that did not hurt the eyes. While many NDErs felt they had a body, they had none. Thus, no eyes that the light could affect.

Some NDErs reported an irresistible urge pulling them toward the Light mixed with longing and expectation. Joy, excitement, and anticipation danced within them like light sparkling on rippling water. As they neared the luminosity, peace, and joy told them they were going home. The closer they got the greater happiness filled them.

Caught up in this magnificent radiance, they instantly realized the Light was far greater than simply illumination. It was a Being, an intelligence that intimately knew every minuscule part of them and, like a loving parent, interacted with them on a personal and caring level. In a way that most could not understand or explain, NDErs were acutely aware that the Being had consciousness and mental awareness far beyond anything known on Earth.

Many people equated the luminous light in general terms to a higher Being that left them spellbound. Others referred to the Presence by a specific name related to their understanding of a higher power. While some saw it as a part of their own essence. Whatever they called it, all who went there ecstatically related to it as the creative force of all that is.

The Source overflowed with such amazing power there was simply nothing in this Earthly existence to relate it to. They could search for a lifetime and still not find a way to express what they experienced. There were no words in any language to describe the Light.

Here are a few reports on these persons' realization of the Being within the Light.

Andrew went to the beach with his class to celebrate the last day of high school. He experienced stomach cramps when he went swimming and drowned. Here is what he tells us of his interaction with the Light.

The ringing in my ears and head is gone, replaced by a gentle silence. As if I am in the middle of a redwood forest with a gentle breeze blowing through the tops of the trees. The radiant Light that looks like a thousand exploding suns overtakes the blackness. My retinas should have been burned out by its brightness, but I can stare into the Light, and it doesn't hurt.

"I am in the Light! Oh my God, I am inside the Light. I am the Light!" I look directly into the source of the Light, and it appears to be a human-like form. Like a massive human silhouette radiating with the intensity of thousands of suns. Although I can't remember seeing it before, somehow, I recognize it. The Light speaks to me. The Light—It knows me. The Light knows my name.

Kathi was another teen who had completed her high school years. Later that summer, with more than a bit of pride, she showed a visiting city friend some of the summer pleasures kids in a small town enjoyed. She and another girl took their friend rafting down a nearby river. Kathi was accidentally dumped into a dangerous whirlpool. Because, in her mind, her invincibility was assured, she had not bothered with a life jacket. When the raft folded down the middle, she was abruptly hurled into the whirlpool and quickly connected to the Being of Light.

As I entered the light, I was surrounded by an immediate feeling of ultimate peace, joy and comfort. I was home. I was surrounded by pure love and acceptance. I was fully connected to this peace and love. I wanted to know what to call the light form. It began telling me some of the many names for God that our world cultures use. Whatever the light truly was, I acknowledged it as a pure energy form. I never actually called it God, but I also knew that many people I knew would have called it that.

Viva died in the hospital, during an operation for a severe pelvic infection and disease. She floated out of her body and watched from above as the surgical team went into resuscitation mode to save her. That was when Viva found herself in a dark void. She tells of her experience there, without any action from her.

There was Oneness of incredible dimensional brightness, beauty, majesty. A most Loving Being drew me to Him inviting me in and pointed the Way to the Light. **All** *wisdom and love were conveyed via unheard thought transmissions from that Being. Although the light was, as yet, a far distant point, I immediately directed myself toward it with all earnestness and the conscious goal of uniting with that light. As I approached, the light grew larger, brighter, and more compelling until I was suddenly thrust into it with indescribable speed.*

Now, in the light...for eternity (seemed like), I experienced a sense of being "held," immersed, fully bathed, buoyant, **one with the Light***! A golden light, warmth, embracing, a state of* **all love***, peace, unity. Wisdom from God, at the center, and innumerable others poured into me to teach and explain the immense divinity of His overall plan from the beginning of time to the future.*

Joyce was accidentally hit on the head by a heavy object as she reached up while cleaning her home. As a highly educated woman of science who worked in research, she had no beliefs in God, religion, or spirituality. One can understand her continued existence after death came as a complete shock.

I was a Ph.D. researcher in biophysics and electron microscopy. My interest was fully immersed in science and research on the ultra-structure of cell pathology in organisms exposed to environmental pollutants. I was not interested in spiritual beliefs, an afterlife, God, or religion. I'd never heard of a near-death experiences nor had any interest in what I would have called fantasy.

31

Immediately upon her accident, she went through the tunnel and ended up at what she calls "a Being of Light."

Suddenly, I was beforef a Being of Light. I couldn't see the face, could communicate, but not in words or pictures even—but through some connection of Oneness. Now, I frequently experience that connection in meditation, but I cannot explain it precisely. It is beyond words and other kinds of experiences.

Linda Stewart died after suffering an extensive illness that had lasted for years. Finally, she gave up the fight and learned the wonders of her being instead. I recommend you read her entire account at near-death.com and find out the amazing things that happened to her after her experience.[5]

The light was everywhere and everything, the brightest I had ever seen. It was dazzling beyond description. Brilliant enough to blind, yet I was not harmed.

The light moved over and through me, washing every hidden place in my heart, It removed all hurt and fear, and transformed my being into a song of joy.

The light was the fulfillment of my search, the loving Source of all that exists, the God of truth and unconditional love, the origin of creation.

I stood in the presence of God and was filled with complete knowing: The light was love, and love was God.

There were no limits to the outpouring and I came to the rapturous awareness of the infinite nature of God's love.

There was no place where God did not exist, and I was within God.

The most amazing aspect for those who have had these experiences was to learn that they felt they were *a part of the Light* or *they were the Light*. No discussion or contradictory debate possible; their connection was as much a fact as their existence. They were closer to the Light than a drop of water to the ocean or a hydrogen molecule to the air.

This strange Being of Light NDErs spoke of was more powerful than the energy a black hole spews into the universe. Yet it was a power filled with gentle caring and love.

3

Let There be Love!

Trainloads of sonnets, poems, and songs have been written about love. We are told it makes the world go 'round and cures all ills, and it is hard to argue with that. Some people drive themselves with the erroneous belief that success is a way to prove their worthiness for love and acceptance. We know little babies who don't receive love literally give up on life and die; the name for this phenomenon is "failure to thrive."

Love in the physical world can be parental love, romantic love, love for family members, or a pet. There's also the love of a wonderful friend who can feel closer than a sibling and even the love of specific objects and activities of life.

NDErs tell us of another incredibly special type of love felt only after we leave this life. Love in the afterlife was such a constant element of the near-death experience that this book could easily have been written on that topic alone. The love felt on the other side of life was so completely enmeshed with the spiritual reality it was inseparable. Like a sweet child curled up on a lap, love poured forth unbidden and intensely welcome. Those who trekked into eternity felt as though they had become tenderly embraced by an adoring parent.

Love is the tether that binds the soul to the Source. It was such an integral part of the Being of Light that it was closer than the radiance from the Light. It was as close as the molecules of living organisms or the electrons of an atom—an inseparable, intricate part of the Being of Love. The love NDErs encountered was as much an actual element of the Light as our hearts and brains are to us.

Once more, as with the Light, those who had the experience struggled and stumbled as they grappled to explain something too overwhelming for words. Others used glowing terms as they expressed the unconditional love they had encountered. Some said there were no words to describe that love because the language had not yet been invented. It was like trying to explain what orange or purple felt like or the sound of brown. The only expression that came close was tears of joy. One individual explained that language was faulty because he was talking the language of the soul, and the world does not have words to attain that level. Indeed, more than one person said that to explain it seemed to depreciate and mar the experience.

We will visit some people and learn what they say as they try to explain the frustration of describing this aspect of their journey. As one person said,

"There are no words to accurately describe the intensity of the experience—words are limiting and seem to minimize something that is beyond the boundary of words. It's hard to get across the penetrating love, warmth, and "HI" feeling. I used to get extreme emotion when discussing it. I can't seem to recapture the incredible events and feelings that happened to me with mere words."

Annie was on her way to classes at college one morning when a driver fell asleep at the wheel, crossed over to her side of the road, and crashed into her car. Without reason or understanding, she abruptly found herself floating out of her body, unsure of what was happening. From her position in the air, she saw her car entangled in an accident and understood. Off in the distance, she saw her college and immediately cried out, *"Oh my God, I can't die now. I still need to finish my finals!"* Slowly, she lowered herself close to the accident and was shocked to see her lifeless body sitting in her car. And then, she tells us,

The air above me drew my attention away from the tragedy and shifted into an awareness of peace and love, which securely embraced every aspect of my being. There was stillness about the atmosphere, holding peacefulness.

There was not only reflected peace, but the fundamental nature of peace was secure in a profound Love that embraced every invisible molecule of air.

The unconditional Love became more concentrated; the awareness filled my inner consciousness with joy, comfort, and ecstasy.

Every cell was gently caressed in the all-abundant Love, that honored and glorified every bit of Who I Am. The Love flowed without conditions or effort; omnipresent and very Real! Love abundantly poured without restrictions, conditions, or commitments.

Ego's constant habit of self-sabotage was nonexistent at last. The veil which separated me from experiencing the Reality of Unconditional Love was effortlessly dissolved. It

Created a Love-based Matrix from within me, and I viewed the Reality of Unconditional Love from the viewpoint of Spirit rather than ego. Even in my conscious-limited view of Spirituality, there was not even a hint of expectations for results toward anyone going through the Unconditional Love-based dimension.

It's hard for most of us to imagine love strong enough to *"embrace every molecule of air,"* or to understand that *"every cell is gently caressed in all-abundant Love."* The mere thought of that concept brings with it wonder and intrigue.

Anita Moorjani has become very well known as her book *Dying to Be Me* hit the bestseller list. She brought back with her several astounding messages she was delighted to share. She was in the last stages of Hodgkin's lymphoma, a form of cancer, and was uncomfortable with chemotherapy. She worked as a counselor in holistic medicine and opted to use that route of treatment. After almost four years of battling the disease, Anita was literally floating in and out of death when her husband finally took her to the hospital for treatment. By that time, her holistic doctor had given up. On the morning of her death, her husband and mother took over the decision-making regarding her treatment.

At the hospital, the doctors took one look at Anita and shook their heads refusing to admit her. "She's already gone," they told her husband and mother. "You've brought her in too late." But, after much pleading and insistence from her loved ones, the doctors eventually agreed to give Anita one chemotherapy treatment—at least until the death sentence was complete.

While she drifted in and out of death, Anita found it difficult to know whether she was in this dimension or the next. Eventually, she returned to share her breathtaking experience. It was one that left even those who have had an NDE gaping with wonder and delight. We will visit with Anita several times throughout this book. Here, we will concentrate on her message of love.

Then, I crossed over to another dimension where I was engulfed in a total feeling of love.

The Love was awe-inspiring. The overwhelming feelings of Love were in a realm of their own. Love complete, pure, and unconditional like I had never known before; unqualified and nonjudgmental.

It isn't necessary to prove an individual's worthiness to God because we already have it. Each of us is loved as a part of creation. And that is the simple truth. We don't have to do anything, be anything or have anything other than to simply be. Love is automatically ours.

I realized that absolutely anything was possible. We didn't come here to suffer. Life is supposed to be great, because we are extremely loved."

Debi-Sue Weiler's committed suicide. At the time of her death, she had given up all hope of her life getting better and looked forward to the oblivion she believed death would bring. After she died, she was completely amazed by the love sent her way. After all, she had committed suicide. A cardinal sin that was supposed to bring punishment, not love.

The sad thoughts faded, and I was overcome by deep, peaceful joy. It felt like I had left all the cares and concerns that were so much a part of me. They were gone.

What I saw as terrible pain, shame, grief, and lack of love on the Earth no longer hurt me. They had no effect on me anymore. I felt only the joy of the release from pain, shame, and the feeling that I could never care for the ones I loved well enough. That was all lifted from me.

I saw the huge, brilliant light directly before me. What I learned next astonished me. That glowing, golden globe of light was alive! It was an existence. It was a living, aware, loving being.

It was like standing in the sun. But instead of sunshine, **love** *warmed me. It was nothing like anyone had ever seen or felt. Yet, strangely, I knew it only loved. There was no other words close to what I experienced. Pure Love came from that being.*

The Power of Love created by that being was a force, like electricity—I felt it touching everything around it. And Love connected me to everything it touched.

That Being was composed of love created love, emitted love, and directed love. It lived on love. It was Love; Love the Power. Everything in that entire experience with the other Divine Loving Being was pure, good, and powered by "love."

That being knew all of everything I ever was and loved me unconditionally. It didn't just love me, but everything that defined me as myself, unique from any other bit of creation, was wonderful to it. It loved the way I was made. It loved that we were meeting. It loved me with all the love it had in it. Its love overpowered me. I knew that I was precious to it and treasured by it. I was what I was supposed to be and was loved just that way. I was flawless, perfect, and beyond beautiful just as I am.

I was so loved! I was loved completely and as I was, as all I was. Small, hurt, confused, and dead by my own hand, I was cherished and loved. I was precious to it. I reacted with my thoughts of joy in the peace, love, and total acceptance it gave me. I tried to love it back with my little self.

If possible, it loved me more. And I loved it more. A cycle of pure love between us grew. It was like the most awesome, perfect joining of hearts between two beings anyone can imagine. I call it perfect communion.

Bobbi has done a wonderful job explaining her connection with Love and her whole experience. We will also hear more from her. Here, we look at what she tells us of her time with Love.

There were six spirits there. I saw them clearly wearing the clothes of their time on Earth. I didn't know any of them from this life. But instantaneously I knew they all loved me deeply, unconditionally, and knew everything about me. They immersed me in unconditional love.

The greatest emphasis of this experience was Love. I was totally engulfed with a love that was beyond anything in our physical world. No matter how deep an affection we feel for our children, it does not come close to this love. The love I felt was the purest, truest, deepest, and totally unconditional love that could be imagined. It goes way beyond what these words can describe.

When I received this love, it wasn't comprehended by my mind. It was felt by my soul. And that immense feeling of this perfect love shot straight into my heart, as a feeling I experienced. Once I had a taste of it, I was forever changed. It was total bliss. What I've always wanted, and then so much more. I was awestruck that I was so loved. I still am, and I forever will be. This light is the source of the "knock your socks off love."

Later in the research, Bobbi is asked, "Were there one or several parts of the experience especially meaningful or significant to you?" This is her answer:

"LOVE, LOVE, LOVE. This Earthly existence is not our real life. We are not meant to live without spirituality. It is part of who we are."

Children also experience this same overpowering and unconditional love during their experiences. Children's NDEs are interesting because they are often too young to have been influenced by other people's thoughts or feelings about death.

Ray was ten years old when he and a friend were fooling around at school, and he accidentally hit his head. Although he only took a few steps before he passed out and had his experience.

A Being of Light and Love greeted me. It was a brilliant light that absorbed me inside itself. The word Love is far too weak to describe this experience. I became Love—my entire being, every thread of my spirit spread throughout the universe, and became Love times a million billion.

Ashley was also ten and playing with friends when she climbed a tree. That was when one of the boys foolishly set fire to the dry, hay-like grass surrounding the tree. As Ashley stepped back from the heat and fell from the tree, lost a lot of blood, and died.

I experienced contented with a feeling of warmth, love, peace, and serenity. The sensation of not wanting to come back was overwhelming; like, what I would describe as, the feeling a baby might have in its mother's womb: safety, love, and excitement of what was to come.

Lisa drowned at age five when the undertow pulled her out of her mother's arms and into the ocean. She tells us that she felt the love and became Love herself.

Next, I remember feeling the most profound and utter sense of peace I have ever felt. Suddenly, I knew I was completely safe, enveloped, and protected by something I can only describe as all-embracing unconditional love. This love surrounded me; it was everywhere, and, at the same time, it was also me, my innermost essence.

The Being of Light showed me that what was most important in life was the love we felt, the loving acts we did, the loving words we spoke, and the loving thoughts we held. Love was all that was important, because only love was real.

"**A**" was raised under very violent circumstances. Her father and grandfather were extremely abusive to her and also sold her as a child prostitute and used her for child pornography. It's understandable that she grew up with post-traumatic stress disorder and could not sleep because of nightmares; she also equated her abuse with sleep. Over time, she became severely depressed and stopped eating, drinking, and sleeping. Shortly after she was taken to the hospital, she died.

Everything was comprehensible—everything was love. This love was created from light; Love-Light was the basic operating source of everything. It was everywhere and within everything. The reason for suffering was not being aware of this Love-Light. I realized what Jesus was talking about (I think I thought of this because I was Catholic). The Holy Spirit in the Bible is pure Love-Light. This spiritual essence was and is inside me and inside each of us. It's that power that can conquer all darkness. It was so simple and beautiful.

Several people returned after being asked to share with the world what they had learned. The reports of the love felt by NDErs were one of those elements that should be loudly broadcast to the world. There is not a single soul in the world that couldn't gain from this information. The lessons found within near-death experiences are beautiful gifts held out to every soul to own as theirs. The best thing is we do not have to do anything to deserve love and acceptance. It is *already* ours. Nor do we have to die to experience this unconditional love; it is within us, waiting to be discovered. If you are not happy with how your life is going, look to your love toward others to make it better.

Dr. Elisabeth Kübler-Ross, a renowned psychiatrist,[6] spent most of her career researching and working with dying people. She was particularly famous for her identification of the five stages of dying: denial, anger, depression, bargaining, and acceptance. Through her work, she believed, *"The ultimate lesson all of us have to learn is unconditional love, which includes not only others but ourselves as well."*

From these accounts, the Loving Light is a part of us. No matter what kind of personality or ego we have constructed—even the essence of a murderer—is still a part of that Loving Light. In addition, if this same Love is not only our Source but a major part of the reality of our being, then how can we not be Love?

4

What Happens at Death

Tentatively, we reach out to embrace the threatening cloud of change within our lives that we fear will sweep us into an unknown abyss. We are convinced personal change will bring tremors that disturb our stability and symbolize the death of all we have known while removing the solid ground from under our feet. Psychologically, change can represent our own private death.

The young consider death too far away to think about. Yet, it has become the principal entertainment that now inundates society. It influences our movies and television and powers our computer games in an effort to sate a juggernaut of adrenalin addiction. Munitions plants sell death like lollypops, which leads us to endless unanswered ethical questions. And, of course, our individual demise looms over us with an hourglass and sickle.

For centuries, religious leaders have stood before their congregations with a raised finger and warnings of the hell and damnation that is sure to be ours because of the original sins we inherited from our ancestors. As large populations have turned away from these lessons, they have been left struggling with unanswered questions.

Not everyone is fearful of dying; some people reach out to embrace death like a welcomed lover. Those who suffer from disease and pain may find every moment alive is an eternity of torture and look to death as a relief. Others may feel the burden of life too emotionally painful and look to the end of their life as the soothing balm of oblivion. Many others who have been touched by the shroud of death during NDEs also welcome their future demise.

Astounding medical advancements have become the alchemy of the future and created many opportunities to resuscitate patients from death. In an article in Missouri Medicine, September/October 2014, called Near-Death Experiences Evidence for Their Reality, Dr. Jeffrey Long states that approximately 17% of all deaths result in an NDE. In the United States alone, that adds up to 60,000,000 people and is growing every day. The advent of covid and the many mass shootings are bringing those numbers up exponentially.

These people return with astounding stories of wonder and mystery. With sparkling eyes and whispers of awe, they explain that the actual experience of dying was simply a transition. They tell of smoothly stepping from the shore of this life into warm, lapping waters of the ocean of eternity as trouble-free as taking a step. Repeatedly, those who returned from death shared stories that at one moment, they were in their physical bodies with all their normal feelings and sensations, and the next moment, surprised and delighted to discover they were still alive and there really is a life after death. Those who sought oblivion through suicide were astonished to learn they continued after death and there was no oblivion. The subject of suicide will be dealt with in detail in the chapter on that topic.

In North America, death has been treated as an unnatural invader, an enemy to be conquered. Today, like a trickled runoff from melting snow, new understanding is gradually seeping through. Drip by drip, we have opened ourselves to discover that death is far more glorious than we ever thought possible. When we listen to those who have taken the sojourn into that alien world, we realize it was the most beautiful and rewarding experience they have ever known.

The research found that although many elements of the near-death experience were similar no two NDEs were exactly alike. It was as if they were creating a marvelous new existence and had included their own special ingredients. For example, some people immediately saw a light, while others went through a tunnel first and then saw the light. Others had no tunnel and either found themselves floating in dark space or immediately went to various destinations (which we will discuss throughout this book).

Many people responded as though they had packed their bodies and transmitted them through their death experience with them. Reason told them this could not be as they had seen their bodies left in the physical realm. Yet, as though their physical being was a passport, they metaphorically brought them to this land with weird and extraordinarily different rules.

Some people had an irresistible yearning to enter the tunnel. In contrast, others found themselves zipping through a passageway without knowing how they arrived or what waited at the other end.

Almost everyone reported a profound, penetrating peace that wrapped them in secure protection with the understanding there was nothing to fear in this strange existence. True to the variations of these phenomena, some tunnels were a circular swirl of misty gray clouds that opened wide enough for them to float through. Other individuals were being squeezed through a tight aperture as though they were toothpaste pushed out of a tube. Numerous folks compared their flight to astronauts racing through a passageway at speeds beyond physical possibility. In contrast, others were able to stop and sightsee. Most were aware only of the corridor, and some reported seeing different beings within their tunnel. Let us take a brief journey through some of the tunnels people experienced.

Stella was a child hit by a car and watched from above as her body rolled to the side of the street. She floated above her body in the ambulance and knew she was being rushed to the hospital. It seems hard to understand her joy when the ambulance driver lost his way to the hospital.

At that point, I thought I would never get to the hospital, and I was overjoyed! I thought, "But is it already over? How lucky! Wowwww!" I entered the tunnel (which I strangely seemed to know well) and went forward at a high speed toward home. I had no intention of stopping to observe anything in the tunnel, I just wanted to get home.

The tunnel was semi-transparent, and points of light, like distant stars, became rays of irregular lights that looked like the headlights of a car speeding down a curved road. My speed kept increasing until the light could no longer reach me, and the tunnel was one giant, barely discernible curve. Then I was home.

Brian was ten years old on a summer day when the temperatures were screaming hot. He and his brother begged their mother to be allowed to go swimming at a local river.

After enough nagging to probably drive the poor woman nuts, they finally wore her down, and she gave in. The boys did not take long to rush off to join their friends. But instead of going where they promised, the group daringly crept through a fence into the restricted zone to the part of the river where the current was not controlled. There was a reason for that fence— it protected the kids like Brian from a dam whose undercurrent was too strong for him, and he drowned.

Then, I saw a light at the end of the tunnel bursting toward me. My spirit or soul became caught in the Light Tunnel, and I flew through it. I still remember the feeling even today! The only depiction I could give is that the feeling was almost a duplicate of the movie Contact. *When the actress went through the tunnel instantly and could see outside space from her space shuttle. That's what I saw when I zoomed through the tunnel. I could see some of the universe beyond the tunnel's transparency. It was an awesome feeling flying through the tunnel at light speed.*

Many years later, Brian says the experience is so fresh in his mind, that he can remember it as if it happened today. Indeed, this is one of the signatures that stand out throughout the reports people sent. They state they can remember every detail of their experience as well as they did when it happened, even when thirty or even fifty years have passed.

Holly was hospitalized with a miscarriage and was given medication that caused an allergic reaction. She knew her temperature had risen and picked up the thermometer on her night table. Holly did not tell us her temperature, but knew she needed immediate help. Before she could call for a nurse, she simply slipped away.

I found myself sitting in a passage, which seemed strange, because I felt like I should be standing. It was similar to an elevator shaft, yet more curved, like a fast-moving tunnel, or a subway than a shaft. It wasn't very wide, and I was very comfortable sitting there. Although there were no seats, I felt secure sitting in suspension.

The tunnel was surrounded by darkness. This was not surprising for some reason. The blackness appeared to be infinite.

As I flowed quickly through this shaft, I recognized there was a soft, glowing light in the distance ahead. Much like city lights appear long before you can see the city...like a glow reflecting off the darkness.

Bobbi was rushed to the hospital with a serious infection and was in the process of dying. When she did not respond to medications, the doctors decided to perform an operation. They knew it was quite dangerous and from which she might not recover. With that in mind, they proceeded, and she did die. Her explanation of the tunnel is wonderful and clearly explains what she felt.

I was being pulled backward in the direction of the pull and my face was facing the Earth. But I don't recall seeing the Earth. It was like a knowing that I was leaving it. It wasn't that I was in a tunnel. It was that a tunnel was created around me due to the extraordinary speed I was traveling. I remember it when I see the white trail that high-speed jets leave across the sky. The jet created the marks. This was the same. There was no fear of any kind in this experience, even though, at this point, what was happening was strange to me. At this time, I knew I'd left my body and was dead. But I didn't care this happened. I was peaceful.

Not everyone who had an NDE was welcomed via a passageway. As though they were taking a shortcut, an almost equal number of people saw no tunnel. Like living in a bubble that popped, they instantly found themselves at their destination. The descriptions of these locations were as richly varied as marbles in a sack. Several people talked about a beautiful garden with colors and plants they had never seen before. Others were instantly surrounded by a gentle glove of perfect velvet blackness before moving on to a white light. Some folks mentioned music that was so beautiful it made their heart sing with its splendor.

As though they were receiving a generous gift, everyone's bodily senses became boosted as they reported the vast improvements. Superman had nothing on them as they discovered they had become far superior to what they had been before death. Those who were deaf or blind in the physical world could hear and see with an acuteness much sharper than anyone on Earth had ever known. It was amazing to discover that, better than a housefly on the wall, they could see in all directions at once and hear numerous conversations simultaneously while understanding all of them. People with various disabilities while in their Earth bodies were thrilled to be whole again.

With the wonder of a child, NDErs were fascinated to communicate through telepathy as concepts entered their awareness complete and whole. Thoughts flooded them at faster-than-lightning speed while every facet of the subject came through as a clear and perfect representation of what was being told. It was as if they had jumped into a swimming pool of information that instantly brought them complete understanding. Once NDErs adjusted to this form of communication, they found it comprehensive and produced more thorough and instant awareness than they had been used to. It was as if they had immediately ingested whole oceans of information on each subject.

Most NDErs were greeted by spirit entities they were sure they had never seen before. Yet, in a way they could not explain, these unfamiliar souls seemed as well-known and close as a beloved family member or dear friend. These entities became guides to this strange world, taking their charges at the speed of thought to a glorious garden or a brilliant city of crystal or gold. Others arrived on mountaintops or gently floated in a soundless black void permeated with love and serenity. Large numbers of people were instantly surrounded by a brilliant white light.

As though they had become visiting relatives, the majority of the NDErs were disappointed to discover that they had to return to their bodies. They reacted to being sent back as though they were being sent to prison for a life sentence. They repeatedly pleaded, begged, and cried not to return to the physical world. Still, most willingly returned once they understood the importance of their continuing bodily existence.

Upon arriving back in their bodies, many NDErs experienced a deep depression. They became homesick for the place they had been. Like starving people, they longed to return to the love they had found beyond this life.

Some people tried to share their experiences with others and were told not to tell anyone because the world would think they were crazy. Others were told it was just a dream or caused by the medications they were given or perhaps hallucinations. Today, many people within the medical profession and the general public have become more open to exploring information from NDEs.

Let us look at the near-death experience in greater detail and find the hidden message waiting for us.

5

Universal Elements

The death experience is like fishing in a rowboat on a beautiful day. We throw our line into the water, lay back, and soak in the rays, with no idea what we will catch. Hopefully, whatever comes up will be recognizable as a fish with gills, a flat tail, and fins.

This scenario can be likened to NDEs in that each is different yet the same. I call the sameness 'universal elements' and are shared by a high majority of people. The list is quite long and could be a book on its own.

Here, we will have a quick look at them. While some experiences are truly universal, others are included because of the numerous reports about them. Several of these points also have a full chapter elsewhere within this book.

Our existence in this material world brings certain things we all share. Every one of us must sleep, eat, and move. These elements of life are a part of being human. In the same way, aspects of the spirit's existence just come with the package and are universal.

The cases I refer to here are those who had positive experiences. Negative events are dealt with in the chapter on Hell and Evil later in this book.

The following is a list of the universal elements of the soul:

Continued Existence

From our worldly perspective, when we see a body, that person is gone. We watch a movie or the news and see a body; in our minds, that person no longer exists. Even if we have been taught otherwise, dead people are dead. Thus, the consciousness of that individual should be a total blank. Yet, NDErs tell us that after death, they are still themselves. They think, feel, and act the same as when they were in the body. They universally return with coherent, logical reports of life beyond.

No Bodies

NDErs often talk about seeing their bodies as a shell the soul used while alive. Yet, throughout their NDE, many talk about themselves as though they still have a body. They walk, hug, eat, and continue reacting like they have a body. (While this is not universal, it is very common.)

Disabilities

Without a body, disabilities are not possible. They look at the brightness of the Light, and it doesn't hurt their eyes because they don't have eyes. They move, see, and hear things they couldn't in the physical world.

Deaf or blind people correctly report specific sights and sounds that occurred during their NDE.

Genders

It stands to reason that without a body, there are no genders. The soul is pure energy and does not need to reproduce; thus, there is no sex. Additionally, genders are limiting, and the soul has no limits.

Communication

Telepathic communication is the way to go at the spirit level. It is extremely rapid because the messages are full concepts instantaneously flashed back and forth. It's also possible to hear multiple conversations simultaneously and understand them all.

Home

Universally, NDErs regard the spirit dimension as home. This is where they belong. Some have memories of being there at some time in the past.

See and Hear Us

While at the spirit level, they can see and hear us. They know what their loved ones are thinking, feeling, and doing. During the NDE, they can be more aware of us than we are ourselves.

Forgiveness

No matter what the issue is, during the NDE, all anger, resentment, and disappointment disappear. They understand the problem completely from all sides, including why something happened. Those of us left behind may continue to carry bad feelings, but for them, it is gone.

See 360°

Spirit is energy. Thus, it makes sense that they can see in every direction simultaneously and understand all they are seeing. Whoa, cool.

Time

Without exception, NDErs report that time and space don't exist. Our physical existence is so enmeshed with time and space that it is next to impossible to visualize life without them.

Confusion reigns because NDErs share their experiences sequentially, which indicates time and space. The reason for this is that *each person creates their own NDE experience* Thus, they generate what they are most familiar with, time and space.

Another reason they explain their events in sequence is because of human language. When we tell of more than one event, we automatically report them in succession, even if it differs from how they were experienced.

Travel by Thought

This next point closely follows behind the tail of time and space. If at the spirit level, time or space don't exist, then it is logical that NDErs could have the illusion of instant travel in any direction. When they were simply placing our attention in that direction.

Love

Without exception, everyone is engulfed in more unconditional love than they can explain. We are told that no words exist in any Earthly language that can express this love. We have already covered the chapter on Love, and there is no need to elaborate here.

Light

NDErs see a Light that repeatedly brings them to a state of awe. They are entranced and know it's far greater than a simple light. A chapter on the Light has also been shared above.

Universal Connection

Without fail, every NDEr returns, experiencing an unmistakable connection to the universe. No matter their individual factors, they all tell of the Oneness.

Universal Knowledge

This element is one of my favorites. I love learning and am thrilled to discover I will be filled with total knowledge. Some people say each question is instantly filled with an understanding of the question, including all the ramifications that connect to it. Others say that without prompting, they are instantly filled with complete knowledge of every question that could be asked.

No Fear of Death

After an NDE, there is no fear of death. Indeed, those who have died welcome it. They want to return to the beautiful place of love.

More Real than Here

Everything at the spirit level was brighter, clearer, and more real than this existence. Some said after experiencing the other dimension, here was not real. This existence seemed more like pretending.

Level of Awareness Sharper

Not only is it more real there than here, but their perceptions are also highly enhanced. No matter what they saw, felt, or experienced, it is heightened compared to here. This existence is dull and dark in comparison.

Definitely Real

The NDERF questionnaire asks participants if they feel their experiences are real or resulting from another cause. Without exception, everyone says their experience was definitely real. This response included those who didn't believe NDEs were real before their experience.

Colors/Music

Although this is not universal, so many people talk about the magnificent colors and the glorious music. These elements should at least be mentioned here.

Other beings

Experiencers tell us they meet other beings while on the other side. Sometimes, it's loved ones or distant relatives who died before them. At other times, it is a guide or even a deity from their religion.

God

Some say they saw God as an old man on a throne. They tell of sitting in his lap and their ecstasy and bliss. However, they are in the minority. Most saw the Light as the Source of all we know. And everyone, without exception, returns clearly stating there is a higher power.

Life Review

We are repeatedly told no outside force or being judges us during the life review. They universally report we are the judge and jury.

Added Abilities

Many NDErs tell us they return with psychic abilities. More detailed information on this is covered in the chapter on Returning.

Personality changes

Having an NDE is a life-changing event. No one returns the same person they were before it began. Most return with strong social, material, and spiritual values.

Spiritual values

Along with personality changes, there have been changes in their spiritual values as well. They may or may not change religions, but how they see their faith is quite different than before. Without exception, everyone, including atheists, returns clearly stating there is a God or higher power.

Returning

A high majority do not want to return. This topic is covered more thoroughly in the chapter Returning. I want to point out that it belongs with universal elements.

Relationships

Their relationships also change because of the great changes in NDErs after their return. Some friends or loved ones can't relate to NDErs' new way of being and drift away. Others became closer, and the relationship was stronger.

Materialism

NDErs no longer gave the same value to material things. They have no interest in a big house or a new car. Any ambitions from before no longer matter. These changes may cause issues with their partners.

6

Were They Really Dead?

The preparation for this book sent me scurrying here and there, poking my nose into crevices and cracks for research information and answers to people's questions. Several people have asked me if NDErs were truly dead. They wondered, were they simply on the edge of death and their brains were still operating. Or could the near-death experience be a case of lucid dreaming? (Simply put, lucid dreaming happens when a sleeping person is dreaming while consciously aware that they are dreaming. They are usually extremely vivid and life-like. In some cases, the dreamer can control what happens within the dream.)

James said this of his NDE,

"I'd like to point out that whoever coined the phrase near-death experience probably never had one. I can assure you there is nothing halfway or near about dying, even if you are fortunate enough to come back from such an experience, dying is quite absolute."

Some people find it difficult to accept that a person could be dead and come back with full-blown memories of events that happened while dead. I can understand their skepticism because, for so long, we have been told by those who know better than us what can or cannot be. As a theology student told me, to her knowledge, only one person died and returned to life. Perhaps she forgot about Lazarus.

Since Dr. Raymond Moody first published his book, discussions have revolved around the validity of the events reported by NDErs. In writing that book, he stepped out of the conservative world of medicine to report his findings without knowing what the reaction of his colleagues would be.

Fortunately, more and more health professionals have an unbiased concept of the near-death experience. On the NDERF website, several scientists, physicians, nurses, and other medical professionals talk of their personal experiences with death.

To answer the question of death or no death, I have brought you a few cases where the individuals involved were clearly dead. In some cases, they were sent to the morgue before they returning to life.

The subject of skepticism is covered later in this book. At this point, we are not talking about doubters but establishing that the individuals having the NDE were, in fact, dead. It's assumed that if a person awakes in various states of rigor mortis, that they have been positively pronounced dead.

We don't have a name for this first gentleman who died in an accident on his farm. He managed to make it from the mishap to the farmhouse before he collapsed. An ambulance was immediately called, but he died in the hospital. After arguing about having to return, he eventually came back to tell us his experience.

I heard this wonderful, familiar voice say, "It is not yet your time to come here. You must go back." I begged it to please not send me back. That is when it told me I had a mission to do. Then, I requested it to please tell me the assignment so I could get it done and come right back. The voice told me I had to return and perform my mission when the time came. I could not know what it was until that time. Then it would be my time to be there.

When I awoke in the hospital the doctor told me I should be dead. That I was going to be buried in a few hours. It had been two and a half hours of death for me. I was cold and stiff as rigor mortis was setting in.

Jack died when he accidentally drove his motorcycle off a cliff. He was rushed to the hospital, where he was pronounced dead on arrival, and his body was sent to the morgue. We'll let Jack take the story from here.

During the two hours and fifty-four minutes that I was dead, I spent one hundred and fifty-five very active and healthy years creating art and architecture on 'the other side.'

When the hospital orderly was zipping me into a body bag in cold storage, I took a renewed breath of life and was back in my physical body.

Rosemary was a twelve-year-old girl who had spinal meningitis. After a week of running a constantly high temperature, she was sick and tired of feeling cold, a tactic hospitals use to bring down fever. Rosemary covered herself with a terry cloth robe, which raised her temperature over the top, and she died. Here, she had just returned to her body from an average NDE.

I heard my surroundings gradually become louder as I slowly returned to my body. However, there was one problem; I was as stiff as a board and could not move. Obviously, I had been gone a very long time, and my body wasn't functioning. Everything hurt like I had a million pins sticking into me. My legs hurt the most as my blood began to flow again. I later learned that our blood thickens after death. This was why I felt so much intense pain. It was like my blood was frozen and was defrosting.

Unfortunately, she does not know how long she was gone.

Patti isn't clear what brought about her death except to tell us that she had given birth to her second child and, for some reason, lost a lot of blood. It was 1952, and the medical profession did not have the knowledge, equipment, or CPR skills it has now. When the doctor saw the blood loss and realized Patti's heart had stopped, she was aware that the physician simply gave up on the mother and worked on the baby. As Patti's soul left her body, she could hear the doctor.

I heard the doctor say she had lost me. I was losing too much blood, and she wasn't able to not stop it. She remarked, "If anyone knows how to pray, they better do it fast." From the doctor's perspective, my vital signs were gone, and she pronounced me dead. While one nurse stayed by my body, the doctor went outside to my family. She asked what they wanted done with the body, as she could not save me.

Patti was greeted by the white Light and a spirit guide who came to talk to her. The next thing she knew, she was again in the hospital outside the delivery room.

While at the spirit level I spoke the words "I choose to live," meaning return and live my life in this body, there was an explosion of light in the room. I had also spoken the same words simultaneously from my body. This caused huge activity among the medics there, as they rushed to my side and began beating on my extremities and heart area to bring back the circulation and start my heart and breathing. Later, I had bruise marks on my body from their efforts to restart the circulation again. Four hours later, I awoke in my room with five doctors and nurses looking at me. My doctor said, "You've really given us a scare."

Dr. George Rodonaia was an avowed atheist when he was hit by a car in his homeland of Russia. At that time, he was a medical doctor and a PhD in neuropathology. When his accident happened, he worked as a research psychiatrist at the University of Moscow.

George had one of the most amazing death experiences ever recorded. When he was hit by the car, he was immediately killed. Upon his arrival at the hospital, his body was sent directly to the morgue. He had been in the morgue for three days when an autopsy began. The moment the doctor cut into him, George was quickly shoved back into his body and returned to life. His NDE is extensive, and anyone who wants to read the full account can find it on the NDERF website or enter George's name into a search engine; there is a long list of connections to him. Because his experience was so amazing and the learning within it so wonderful, I have included a little more than just his return. Here are the highlights of his NDE.

The first thing I remember is that I was in total darkness, yet still somehow aware of my existence as George. I was horrified! I was shocked to find I still existed. The one thought in my mind was, "How can I be when I'm not?" That is what troubled me. Then I remembered Descartes' famous line: "I think, therefore, I am." And that took a huge burden off me for it was then I knew for certain I was still alive, in a very different dimension. Then I thought, "If I am, why shouldn't I be positive?"

At this point, George was greeted by the Light, where he spent quite a lot of time.

So, there I was, flooded with all these good things and this wonderful experience, when someone began to cut into my stomach. Can you imagine? What had happened was that I was taken to the morgue, pronounced dead, and left there for three days. As they began to cut into my stomach for an autopsy, I felt as though some great power took hold of my neck and pushed me down. And it was so powerful that I opened my eyes with this huge sense of pain. My body was cold, and I began to shiver. They immediately stopped the autopsy and took me to the hospital, where I remained for nine months, most of which I spent under a respirator.

After his experience, Dr. Rodonaia went on to get a PhD in the psychology of religion and became a priest in the Greek Orthodox Church until he moved to the United States. There. he served as an associate pastor at the First United Methodist Church in Nederland, Texas. In October 2004, Dr. George Rodonaia died for the final time of a massive heart attack.

Mandy went to the hospital to have gallstones removed when something went wrong, and she died. While her story is short, it makes the point that she was indeed dead. Mandy suddenly found herself outside her body and was met by her deceased family members. Later, she talked to a higher being and felt the deep love common to the NDE. Mandy tells us that at that point, she wanted to stay where she was, but it was not to be. She was clearly told she had to go back; this is what happened next.

The next thing I knew, I was sucked out of this wonderful place. As I returned, I saw my doctor hitting my chest and praying to the Lord to help him bring me back. Later, I asked him about that, and he inquired how I knew that because he was saying it to himself.

That short minute and twenty-five seconds was more wonderful than my whole life here. It was the most incredible experience I've ever had.

Nadir was speeding in a car with a group of friends as they headed to a football game. They were excited because their favorite team was playing. He was sitting in the window with his legs inside the car and the top half of his body sticking out of the rear window. That is when he noticed an animal or the road, and they got into an accident trying to avoid the creature. Nadir says he pulled himself into the car but was killed in the accident anyway.

Nadir's experience is important to include here; however English is not his mother tongue. I have edited his report while keeping his meaning intact.

It felt like I was so tall, yet my body had no weight. Immediately, I saw my life from the moment of my birth until the accident. Then, I began walking and noticed others around me. Some looked like they were waiting for something from me. There was many people I had mistreated or hurt, and they were looking at me as if they wanted to take revenge.

Suddenly, I came to a stop, although there was a long road and another world before me. I felt very cold; I didn't know why. Then, I was falling from a high cliff, yet I didn't feel the impact of the ground—everything was dark. I knew I had returned to my body. I tried to stand up and turn around but I kept hitting myself on something hard surrounding me and fell. It was very cold, and I tried to stand again. That's when I saw a light and the face of a man staring at me. The man ran from me like a lion was running after him. Do you know who that man was? He was the person who was responsible for burying the dead [the mortician]. *I learned after my recovery that I'd been dead for about thirteen hours.*

Diane was in an auto accident and was thrown from the car. While she was lying on the ground, she felt herself being gently held by a man. He spoke to her and told her that she would be all right. She was fascinated that his words were heard telepathically. When she asked him who he was, he told her, "I'm just a drover."

Let's join Diane as she is waking up in the morgue.

When I awoke in the morgue, I was naked and paralyzed. The only available light came from the opaque glass window of a door. Two people stood in the doorway; a nurse holding the clothes I had been wearing and my brother-in-law. He said, "Do dead people cry." The nurse looked at me and said, "Oh, my God."

At that point, Diane was taken to intensive care. She also tells us that while out of her body, she went to the waiting room where her family was and became annoyed at the conversation she heard.

My Mom, sister, and brother-in-law were there. My sister asked, "I wonder if we should stay?" My brother-in-law said, "I'll do whatever you guys want." Mom said, "Well, you know I don't like hospitals."

Later, my sister and brother-in-law verified both the conversation in the morgue and corridor. Eventually, years later, an aunt told me that her grandfather, my great-grandfather, always said of himself, "I am just a drover."

While these experiences are interesting, they are not the only way to know that NDEs are real. A high number of people return with information they should not know. They may know that a friend or relative has died while no one else is aware. They meet relatives or deceased siblings they didn't know about. Or they may bring back personal information about another that they couldn't possibly know.

In 2014, Dr. Jeffrey Long wrote an article specifying ways to know if a report actually happened.[8] He tells us that these people are dead or in a coma and should not have any cognitive activities. Yet they come back with clearly stated events that fit a pattern shared with others who have died.

Young children aged five and below have the same experiences as older individuals. These kids are too young to have been strongly affected by adults or society. Yet they also follow the same pattern of experiences as others.

Evidence of death weaves its way through people's experiences. The hospitals where these events occurred would have medical reports supporting these claims.

Numerous people died and returned to describe the proceedings around them accurately and vividly report them in great detail. Whether they died in an accident or during an operation. They are able to talk about who came and went, what actions happened, and who said what. They also reported highly personal information of those in the vicinity.

Studies by Dr. Michael Sabom[9] have been done with these individuals to test the accuracy of what they reported. Repeatedly, people with NDEs could accurately describe the efforts of the people trying to work on them. Those who had not died could only guess (often erroneously) what might be done to them during their operations. We will see more validation of NDEs throughout this book.

7

Doubters

Doubts and questions are as important to us as sunlight to a plant. Sincere responses to doubts are the glue that holds the reality of these reports together. It helps us to put things into perspective and separate facts from imagination. Doubters' questions force us to find ways to show that NDEs are indeed a real phenomenon.

Dr. Wilder Penfield pioneered brain research and conducted several tests on the human brain that have become very well known.[10] During the 1940s and 1950s, he and his colleagues did groundbreaking treatment of individuals with epilepsy. While the patient was awake, Dr. Penfield stimulated parts of the patient's brain. The patient then recalled memories from their past in infinite detail. Dr. Penfield died in 1976 without making any comment on NDEs. Yet some have seen his work as an explanation for the near-death experience.

Dr. Susan Blackmore, for many years, has worked hard at debunking the reports of near-death experiences. She saw it as the neurons losing blood flow in the brain. Dr. Kevin Nelson, a University of Kentucky researcher, agreed with Dr. Blackmore and felt that the NDE was simply the result of hallucinations that happen during the dying process.

Dr. Tomasz S. Troscianko, and Dr. Blackmore, speculate, "If you started with very little neural noise and it gradually increased, the effect would be of a light at the center getting larger and larger and hence closer and closer....The tunnel would appear to move as the noise levels increased and the central light got larger and larger," Here, Dr. Troscianko is talking about the Doppler effect, the process of sound when a vehicle is coming at you and then passes. While the car is approaching, the sound becomes higher and higher in pitch. The sound is higher on the scale at the exact point it reaches you. It instantly switches as it passes to become a lower and softer sound. Dr. Troscianko felt that this sound sequence would explain the tunnel many people experienced. Given the tunnel experiences we have learned about here, the Doppler effect would be a poor explanation. It doesn't define the other aspects of NDEs, including those who had no tunnel.

An experiment was tried by Dr. Karl Jansen[11] when he reproduced some of the effects of the NDE by giving his patients the drug ketamine. It was very difficult to get unbiased information relating to ketamine and NDEs. However, it seems ketamine has some similar aspects of the death experience. It appears to produce an OBE (Out-of-Body Experience), which isn't an NDE. There is no Loving Light Being, overwhelming love, or other elements present in an NDE.

Indeed, each one of these explanations has spoken to some of the specific *segments* of the NDE. One may comment on the light, another on the tunnel experience, and another on the effects caused by drugs. Yet, their explanations have not been able to debunk the full experience in their explanation. What about travel by thought, telepathic communication, Oneness, or huge blocks of knowledge, to name a few. Nor have they been able to respond to the amazing lessons being brought back.

There are over twenty explanations for NDEs. Some say NDEs are the brain's neurons shutting down during death or perhaps due to false memories. Still, others suggest the experience is a lack of blood to the brain, the brain's reaction to danger, and even a craving for God in the person's life. Many erroneously equate the NDE phenomenon to parapsychology, new-age crystal gazing, and even the field of mediumship.

These explanations are only hypotheses. Above, I said I appreciated critics, and I do. But they must back up their theories with facts. Where is the research? Indeed, there should be multiple research projects to verify these claims. What about peer review? Nope, none of that either.

Generally, the medical profession is very conservative and insists on many experiments to ensure the claims are real. Yet, in the case of NDEs, the medical profession has grabbed onto these hypotheses as fact and run with it, calling it reality.

From their perspective, it is not very clear. NDEs are something that happens because of death or near death and belong to that discipline. However, from a pragmatic perspective, there are no explanations. Thus, it's understandable that some doctors dismiss them because they cannot be put through the same tests used for medical research.

Let me assure you that near-death experiences have nothing to do with the supernatural or the spooky-wooky world. NDEs like those talked about where people have been sent to the morgue and revived don't fit any of the doctor's explanations.

There are over twenty different skeptic explanations to the near-death experience. Indeed, they illustrate the creativity of the human mind and fit better into the area of human curiosity that has us tearing apart things until we understand them. These erroneous explanations are people reaching to answer that which they do not understand.

Several studies have been done to establish the truth of near-death experiences using scientific methods. Understanding the NDE is as difficult as catching a bird in flight because the scientific method requires that an experiment be repeated repeatedly under highly monitored and controlled conditions to arrive at the same results each time. As you have seen in the NDEs offered above, arriving at the same conclusion each time does not happen.

Establishing proof of the existence of the soul and the truth of the near-death experience is also an interest of Dr. Jeffrey Long and his wife, Jody Long. It was to confirm the validity of NDEs that they set up NDERF (Near-Death Experience Research Foundation) website. Since 1998, they have collected thousands of NDEs. Dr. Long has since written two books and many articles on the subject.

After reading 2,500 NDEs, I, too, find it hard to believe that they are not true death experiences. In fact, as Dr. Raymond Moody pointed out in 1975, so many of the stories were alike that he wondered how so many people could have such similar experiences without collaboration.

Still, the methods used do not come close to the rigid controls required to validate NDEs as scientifically true. All the reports given are anecdotal and are considered hearsay.

Once more, here are some near-death experiences that get very close to the proof that is being sought.

Cate died when the medications she was taking disagreed with one another. After feeling the peace and love, she, like many others, resisted returning and found it difficult to settle into her body; she constantly felt she was half in and half out of it. Then, Cate met with two young men from the other dimension she had met during her experience. These men helped her understand it was not her time.

In a moment, I felt the presence of two other deceased souls. I discovered they were two young men from this lifetime who had recently died from a tragic car accident. They told me details, such as, their names, the location, and the circumstances that were a part the accident. They repeated that I still had things to learn in this life.

Later, I went on the Internet and began searching for the car accident in the news. After a few minutes of searching, I saw a picture of the same young man who had recently died in a car crash with his friend. I felt chills go up and down my spine because the name, the location, and circumstances around the accident, along with his picture corresponded exactly with what they had told me.

Gregory was in the middle of a heart attack while playing basketball with a friend, an emergency room doctor. When he told his friend his symptoms, he was not taken seriously and was asked to play two more games instead of acting. After the games, with the help of the gym manager, he eventually made it to a medical clinic across the street, only to find it closed for lunch. The gym manager finally called 911 and got help. While in the hospital, Gregory died and witnessed the following scene.

I opened my eyes, and from above I saw Ann, my wife, sitting at the foot of my hospital bed, looking at me. A blond nurse entered the room and she tripped over Ann's feet trying to get to the other side of my bed. The nurse raised her left hand, and I noticed she had a watch with a brown strap. She hit me in the chest, which caused me to reenter my body.

A few minutes later, Gregory left his body a second time and witnessed the following:

This time, I watched a brunette nurse with shoulder-length hair come into the room. She took my wife by the shoulder and said, "Mrs.___, you need to go now." The nurse took Ann to a lounge-like place. The same blond nurse came into my room with a different, taller, brunette nurse, together with my doctor and an Asian doctor. A few moments later another nurse entered the room. I watched this activity as if from a wide-angle view that looked directly down on those in the room. At first, it felt like I was still mortal. As a joke I asked the Chinese doctor why he hadn't plugged the bald place on top of his head, considering all the money he made. When no one laughed, I realized they couldn't hear me.

Still later, after they got him stabilized, he was put into another room with several other beds.

I was placed in ICU. My doctor said my heart had stopped three times. "No! Just twice," I corrected him. "The first time, that blond nurse standing beside you came in and tripped over my wife's feet while rushing to get to me. She hit me on hard on the chest, and I came back. The second time a brunette nurse took my wife out, then you and a Chinese doctor with a bald spot on the top of his head came into the room. There were five people in the room working on me that time." At that point, my doctor appeared disturbed by what I had said and left. The blond nurse was shocked at what I had told them.

Doctors' reactions to NDEs are changing. In the past, too many doctors have either walked away, refused to talk about the subject, or even become frightened. Today, more are listening to their patients and becoming more open about the near-death experiences.

Tom was allergic to insect bites and was stung by a nest of wasps. He went into anaphylactic shock and died. He tells us this is what happened.

I was aware of my existence and knew I was still me. I saw the surgical team removing blood from one arm and put fresh blood into my other arm while they administered adrenalin. The moment I was resuscitated, I returned to my body.

The next day, as I thought about the supernatural phenomena I had just experienced. I wondered how I could analytically verify my experience. The ER orderly was passing by and saw I was awake. I asked him, "Why were you putting blood into one arm while taking it out of the other?"

Surprised, he replied, "How the hell did you know we did that? You were gone?"

So many people have died and witnessed the events happening where they are, that it is impossible to list them here. Suffice it to say that the numbers are in the millions. Why aren't they being acknowledged? Logically, they should not be able to know any of this information. Their bodies are lying on the operating table, and they are unconscious or dead. How can they know about anything going on in the room? The same can be said for people who die in accidents away from hospitals. They too know all the activity going on around them.

Dr. Sabom, a cardiologist living in Georgia, interviewed one hundred patients who had an NDE. He wanted to distinguish if these patients were using a creative imagination or had accurate knowledge of what happened in their hospital room. Sixty-one people reported a classical NDE while also witnessing events in the room. These patients gave detailed descriptions of what happened in the operating room while they were supposed to be dead or dying.

To be thorough in his investigations, Dr. Sabom interviewed a group of cardiac patients who had not experienced near-death. He asked them to imagine being resuscitated by a medical team and describe what they thought those steps would be. The doctor was amazed to discover that eighty percent of that group could not accurately explain the procedure. While those who claimed to have viewed what happened during an NDE were completely accurate in the details and equipment used.

The Human Consciousness Project was a 2008 gathering of scientists and doctors interested in learning more about the human brain and how it operates. In particular, they paid specific attention to the study of the near-death experience. They found that many people who were revived after a cardiac arrest could report clearly, with well-structured thought processes, reasoning, memories, and detailed accounts of the attempt to resuscitate them. Yet consistently these same individuals showed no signs of life and no brain activity; the heart had stopped, and the patient wasn't breathing. Their studies suggested that, in some way, the mind and consciousness continue to function while clinical death is fully present.

I would like to make one point about the brain, mind, and consciousness studies. Although I realize how one can become confused, I do not believe the brain and consciousness are the same thing. Consciousness is that soul of Oneness to which we all belong. Although thought is found in the brain, it is not possible to study the brain and find consciousness. I believe that part of us is found within every cell and even within the DNA of the body.

If mind consciousness is found in the brain, how is it that people whose brains have stopped functioning can come back to tell of exact details of things they could not possibly know? How do people return with information they should not possibly know? How can blind people return with detailed descriptions of things they have never seen while in their bodies? Where is the research on these cases?

Dr. Kenneth Ring is well known for his work with the near-death experience and blind people. In their 1999 book *Mindsight*[12], Dr. Ring and Sharon Cooper tell of interviews they had with thirty-one blind people who had an NDE. Every one of these people reported that they could see, and that the clarity stood beyond their expectations.

Dr. Raymond Moody's book, *Life After Life,* is responsible for starting a maelstrom of interest and controversy around the world on the subject of NDE. Was what Dr. Moody saying true, or had he misunderstood? He says the scientific community was very supportive of his work. This is because, despite the title of his book, Moody never once made the claim that the people he interviewed had actually died. Since that time, he has gone on to publish several books related to the topic of the NDE.

Near-death experience.com is an excellent website that boasts a large selection of well documented and scientific studies on the NDE. A section called "Scientific Evidence of Survival" offers serious seekers outstanding information. In addition to providing stories of hundreds of near-death experiences, the site also has a large selection of investigative evidence. Here are some interesting examples from that site of people knowing things they could not know because they were clinically dead at the time.

An elderly woman, blind since her childhood could see during her NDE. She was able to accurately describe the instruments and techniques used during her resuscitation. After the woman was revived, she stated the details to her doctor. She told the doctor who came in and out, what they said, what they wore, what they did, all of which was true. Her doctor then referred the woman to Dr. Raymond Moody, whom he knew was doing research at the time on NDEs.

In another instance, a woman with a heart condition died at the same time as her sister was in a diabetic coma in different part of the same hospital. The woman talked about a conversation she had with her sister as they hovered near the ceiling and watched the medical team work on her body below. The woman told the doctor that her sister had died while her resuscitation was taking place. At first the doctor denied it. But when she insisted, he eventually had a nurse check on it. The sister had, in fact, died during the time in question.

In this next report, a young woman, **Kathy**, visited her sister in the waiting room while she was dead. She also shocked her doctor with the details of what was happening in the room while he worked to revive her.

Kathy left her body and went into a room in the hospital where her older sister was crying and saying: "Oh, Kathy, please don't die, please don't die."

Then she returned to the operating room and watched her resuscitation.

Later, the doctor said that I had a really bad time. I said, "Yeah, I know."

He asked, "How do you know?"

"I know everything that happened," I told him. When the doctor didn't believe me, I told him the whole story, from when I stopped breathing until I came around. He was very shocked that I knew everything that had happened and didn't quite know what to say. He returned several times to ask me different things about it.

Later, when her sister came to see her, she told her what she had heard. And the sister verified that it was exactly true.

This next woman was in an accident and had an NDE.

When I awoke after the accident, my father was there. I didn't care what shape I was in, how I was, or even what the doctor's diagnosis about my condition. All I wanted to talk about was the experience I had just been through. I told Dad about who had dragged me out of the building, what color clothes they wore, how they got me out, and even the conversations of those in the area were having.

And my father said, "Yes, that's all true."

Yet, throughout my body was completely out this whole time, and there was no way I could have seen or heard these things while being outside my body.

Stella is the child we heard from above who was delighted that the ambulance had lost its way. Her experience is remarkable as she returned with some credible information to show its reality.

Before entering the tunnel, I saw the ambulance nurse lose her ring and where it fell. Later, when came to see me, I told her where to find it without her having asked about it. I knew that the ambulance had gotten lost in a neighboring county and knew who the driver was without having met him. Also, that I had been brought to the hospital in a private automobile.

Maria was operated on and died during the procedure. The doctors revived her and finished their work. Later, when the patient awoke in the recovery room, her doctor came to see how she was doing. During that visit, the woman told the doctor of a tennis shoe she had seen sitting on an outside ledge of the hospital. It was a beat-up blue runner. The lace closest to the building was tucked under the shoe and, from the patient's view, it was hanging down the side of the building.

At the time, the doctor dismissed the woman's claim. She believed the woman could not possibly know of such a shoe. When the patient insisted, the doctor referred her to one of the hospital's social workers, Kimberly Ann Clark. The story bothered Ms. Clark, and she decided to see for herself if there was, in fact, such a shoe. It took her a while, but eventually, she found the shoe on a ledge on the third floor, above the floor the patient had been on. It was a different part of the hospital where this patient had never been. Amazingly, the only way the woman could have known the exact description of the shoe, lace and all, was if she was looking at it from somewhere in the middle of the air.

Doubter may have questions, but these stories show that we are far more than just physical beings wandering around the Earth. In the next chapter, we will look closer at science and how it connects us with Oneness.

8

Life Review

Sometimes, we wish we could magically turn back the hands of time and change things we regret, comments made without thought, uncaring treatment of others, serious neglect, or decisions that changed our lives in directions we never planned to go. Others may look back in pleasure at their lives with a sense of satisfaction they were kind, caring, and giving to others.

Those who have had an NDE tell us time travel was instant while they went through their life review. As though the life they had lived had been plucked out of the ether and flashed on the screen of the universe for their evaluation. As though caught in movie reruns, every aspect of their lives was examined from birth to the time of their deaths. It included film cuts usually left on the screening room floor. Most people were shown in minute details every action and thought they had ever had—good and bad. Others simply slipped through a brief review as though they were watching a movie trailer.

For centuries, we have been taught our actions are judged after death and fitting punishments are meted out according to our sins. Yet not one person who had a life review reported they were appraised, nor were any punishments allocated for their actions. The opposite was more the case. Throughout the life reviews, those having the experiences were embraced in an intense and perpetual shroud of unconditional love and acceptance.

The closest analogy given was that of a small child playing with friends and getting into disagreements. NDErs repeatedly felt that, although they had done something they should not have, they were still deeply loved unconditionally.

Although the life reviews were sometimes uncomfortable, the main purpose wasn't to punish but to help the growth and understanding of those souls doing the inspection. When their actions were motivated by kindness and love, they felt deep joy and satisfaction. And when their actions were unkind and based on selfishness, their pain and sorrow were in equal intensity as the person they had dealt with. Their souls felt great disappointment with their choices. Then, they were asked what had been learned as a result of the life reviews. It was through the realizations brought from the answers to this question that the soul grew.

No matter what actions had been done in life, everyone, without exception, reported becoming their *own* judge and jury. During the evaluation of their lives, one aspect of themselves relived their life moment by moment in real-time, while another stayed back and appraised what was shown. They were concurrently treated to all the pain and sorrow, relief and joy the people they had dealt with felt. Then, as if given the deluxe model, those deeds became a handful of pebbles tossed into calm water. The NDErs saw and felt on an intimate, outreaching, and overlapping level, the consequences their behavior caused for those subsequently touched by the individual who had been helped or hurt. They closely felt the ongoing reactions as though they were themselves the recipient, whether wonderful or painful.

Several people returned to describe their life as an intricate tapestry interwoven with everyone they touched and beyond.

While there was only love and no fires of hell, NDErs did have to face the consequences of their actions. It is beyond conception to consider what the life review must be like for people who have lived a life of inflicting pain and suffering on others. It would be excruciating to feel all the pain they dished out plus, how that reverberated in the world. That would be living one's worst nightmare as they relived every injury repeatedly until the anguish caused finally trickled through and ran out. The world is still feeling the painful backlash from those in concentration camps during World War II, and the effects of that time are still being felt almost 80 years later.

The life review affected those who went through it to the core of their being. Most returned with an entirely changed attitude toward life and a deeper respect for others, the world, and everything in it. They became more proactive in the world and reached out to others in a more positive way.

Here, we look at what some of these people had to say about their experiences.

Amy was a teen who suffered from severe fibromyalgia. The pain was so intense that it prevented her from lying in one position for any length of time. She managed only short naps throughout the night. Amy looked forward to the relief the pain medication offered—until she discovered she was allergic to it. She was torn between the comfort it gave her and her worry over the consequences of the allergy. When she reported her reaction to her doctor, he did not seem too worried, He said it was just her body getting used to the medication and suggested she take a stronger dose. After struggling with a lack of sleep for days, she followed the doctor's advice and died. We pick up her story while she is with her spirit guide.

My guide lovingly supported me throughout my life review. I never felt chastised, even though times I knew I was cruel at times and hurt many people. I had lost my temper in terrible ways and had trouble with forgiveness. Yet, I only felt Love and understanding throughout the entire life review.

That was a big aha moment for me. Throughout my life, I thought that every imperfect action I did was watched "by God" and judged with anger or great sadness. I felt surrounded by constant guilt and repeatedly when over the dread of "being watched" with severe or at least very stern eyes. I was given the opportunity and the gift to stand back and more fully understand and love myself.

I experienced every detail of what others felt because of my treatment. I realized how everything I did and said and even thought touched others around me in one way or another.

I joined the minds and emotional centers of many others to understand their perspective in their thinking. How each one's personal views and life experiences had brought them to the places they now stood. I felt their struggles and fears, their desperate need for love and approval. The chance to view others from a much higher frequency was wonderful.

After my NDE, I was filled with a flood of Love for a woman I'd had issues with. I wrote her and told her how much I loved her and asked for her forgiveness. She could have been my firstborn child. That is how much I adored her.

Leonard had his near-death experience after a heart attack. It was fortunate for him that he was in the hospital at the time. Otherwise, he may not have been around to tell us about what he learned. At the time of his death, he watched from above as people tried to revive him. After a while, Leonard lost interest and decided to wander. He quickly visited his mother's house before suddenly finding himself in space, looking at the Earth like he was in the International Space Station.

God showed me every aspect of my life from birth until the NDE. I felt and experienced all these events once more and intimately felt the emotions I had caused in others. I was the only judge! This experience was very painful. I cannot imagine what Adolf Hitler underwent while feeling the pain of millions of individuals. God showed me times when I had generously done things without thinking about it and when I had done unloving things. I actually saw myself stealing sweets in a shop, and thought, "Whew, nobody saw me!" But somebody did. God saw me! Yet he didn't judge me. In fact, that's what affected me the most: God just loves us unconditionally. The love is indescribable; it's not like anything we feel on Earth. This is rather a love-force.

We met **Bobbi** earlier when she talked about the journey through the tunnel. She was aware that she had died and left her body, but that understanding had little interest to her. It was like a side comment in a conversation. Although the life review can come at any point during the NDE, Bobbi went through the tunnel and met with other souls before she reviewed her life.

Everything was laid bare. Yet there was no shame, guilt, or deceit. It wasn't possible in that place. There was total understanding without ever realizing the thought of needing to understand.

There, at this place outside of the physical body, everything that you are, feel, think, and believe was transparent for anyone to see, feel, and understand with perfect clarity. It wasn't what I did in my physical life that mattered. It was the person I was, who I was inside my soul that was the most important than anything physical that I did. In other words, it was only the kind of person I really was, in terms of my soul. That was most important.

That's not to say that the life experiences hadn't contributed significantly to the person I was. They had. The impact of physical actions on the soul cannot be reduced. It's hard to explain. It was as though we might think that maybe we could do bad things to others or have bad thoughts about them and it would still be okay, as long as we remained a beautiful person. That's completely wrong. Those things do change our souls, and we can do nothing to change that. But physical actions were not as important as the person (me) that those experiences had created.

Later in the questionnaire, Bobbi was asked if she had had a life review. This is what she said:

I learned a great deal. We are a part of one. We should savor life, all life. We don't die. We are freed after physical death occurs. I am not afraid of death, but I thoroughly understand we need to live life. I have a greater respect for life and I'm capable of extraordinary depth comprehension, understanding, and love. Don't hurt others—we are all part of the same Oneness. Don't judge—seek wisdom instead and help others…

There is so much more to life than we realize. This life is way more important that we realize.

We will hear from Bobbi again as she shares her learning with us.

Glauco, a spunky eight-year-old boy, was enjoying one of those summer days that one treasures. The sun was bright, and the air was filled with butterflies and the smell of cornflowers. He and his two older brothers were fishing with their father. It didn't take long before the boys became bored and pleaded with their father for permission to wander along the riverbank. The lads considered themselves very lucky when they eventually wore their father down, and he gave in. But with a strong warning not to go into the water.

The boys had not gone far along the shore when they came to a barrier blocking their progress. After assessing the situation, they concluded that if they wanted to proceed, there was no solution to their dilemma but to enter the water to get around it. Unfortunately, none of them knew how to swim, and when they stepped into the water, they were shocked to discover there was no bottom. Like falling dominoes, each of the children went into the water to save the one before with the same results. Shortly after falling into the deep water, Glauco panicked as he felt his life fade away. His experience is both very informative and charming in his youthfu approach to it.

I heard the most pleasing and kind voice telling me tc relax and that everything would be okay. Then, I felt arms embrace me. I knew it was a man and he was very gentle.

Glauco was then taken to a beautiful, bright light and greeted by a Being of Love. Although he was still a child, he had his life reviewed.

He said he was there to help me with my questions (ana boy, I had lots of questions). Before the questions he showed me my life like I was in a movie. My life went backward. I remember thinking, how bad can it be? I'm only eight years old. Yet the first image was about something bad that I did (I purposely scratched the side of a car). I felt the pain that I caused by my actions. I remember thinking, "Oooh no! I'm in trouble!" Then my angel surprised me and said, "Don't worry; these are just lessons." I thought, "Oh crap, this guy can read my mind too." He heard that, as well, and gave me a lovely, beautiful smile. The movie was showing second by second of my entire life. With every event I saw, I felt the results of it on others. As if, everything I did had a life of its own. Like when I felt the owner of the car's feelings and thoughts. Then he told his wife and I felt her pain too, and on and on and on (not a good feeling).

My angel didn't show me just the bad things I did; he also showed me the things I did out of love. I watched the time I took a homeless boy, I'd become friends with, home with me.

We showered together; ate together, and I gave him some of my clothes. I felt how happy I made my angel. He explained that those were the things that really mattered. They make a difference in the world for the better.

Hafur's experience is stuffed full of meaningful learning as we hear from her again. Her NDE resulted from an unspecified medical condition. As Hafur was moving through her tunnel with a guide, she saw many shadowy people, including a man she thought may have been her grandfather. He was wandering back and forth and around and around with his head down. Floating above him, a guide talked to him, although Hafur could not hear what the guide said. She wanted to speak to him, but her own spirit guide said not to bother him because he was too involved in his own thoughts to pay attention to her. They continued through the tunnel to the end, and Hafur immediately became engaged in her life review.

The figure to my right guided me and stopped by a hill that served as a place to project my life from beginning to end. It was astonishing that my life was shown with events I had completely forgotten. Other events seemed so insignificant that it felt like I was watching a frame by frame of the personal movie of my life on Earth. Everything stood out with great clarity and a heightened lucidness I had never experienced before. I realized that I had personally chosen to take on a physical existence and to have the life experiences I was having. I recognized that I had wasted time in suffering, when what I should have been doing was to use my freedom to choose love and not all the pain that came into my life.

No judging or punishing God existed. My mind, with a vastly expanded consciousness, judged itself and sifted its actions through a filter of perfect, conscious love.

Universal memory records everything, even the smallest things. I had voluntarily taken form in my body and designed the life I would experience. I wanted to learn how to truly love more and better. Everything we do must be done from true love, unconditional and universal without ulterior motives or judgment.

There's only one law and that is life. Death doesn't exist. We are God. It's our own super-lucid consciousness that judges us with love. What we think or want to think is most relevant. This is the way the universe is constructed. Like a game of consciousness that recognizes itself and recreates itself through each of us. While at the same time, we are the "point of nothingness" in which life will become self-aware.

Rick chose an icy cold winter morning to go on a hunting excursion, even though he had just come home after working all night. He was anxious to get going and immediately gathered his things and tramped off to hunt. His wife had already left for work, and Rick did not bother to tell anyone where he was going. After all, he was on his family's property, and knew it well. He was convinced there was no danger. Yet shortly after leaving the house Rick slipped at the edge of a cliff and fell onto some rocks at the bottom of a ravine by a river. His experience strongly affected him, and he wanted to shout it from the rooftops. We pick up his story as he is having his life review.

Then, it suddenly happened! "What have you done with your life?" The voice penetrated my very being to the core. I couldn't answer. I saw what seemed like a movie, on my right, and I was in it. From my birth, childhood, and friends. I saw it all up to my death. I witnessed everything I'd ever done before my eyes. While my life played out, I endeavored to think of good things I had done. Raised in the church, I had been very active in church functions. As I pondered over this, I saw a man in his car who had run out of gas. This was about a year ago. I stopped and took him to a local gas station, bought him gas, as he had no money, and helped him on his way. I thought to myself, "Why am I seeing this?" The voice was loud and clear. "You took no thought to help this soul and asked nothing in return. These actions are the essence of good."

I also saw all the people I'd hurt and was shown how my actions had set in motion the actions of others. I was astonished, I never thought my life influenced the actions of friends, family, and others. I was shown the results of all I'd done. I wasn't pleased with myself! I watched until the events came to an end. In reality, I had done so little with my life. I had been selfish and even cruel in so many ways. I truly was sorry I had done so little.

Andrew had gone with a group of friends to the beach to celebrate their graduation from high school. There, he played games, ate lunch, and immediately went swimming. He no sooner entered the water than his stomach cramped from the shock of the cold. Andrew's concern became serious when the spasms got stronger, and he drowned. He left his body, was sucked through a tunnel, and went straight to a strange Light. While he was in the Light, he had his life reviewed.

Inside the sphere it was like an enormous, unending movie screen. Hundreds of movies were playing in every direction simultaneously. Images surrounded me of all my life experiences from my many lifetimes. Wherever I looked, I saw the events of the lives I had lived. Astonishingly, I could hear, feel, touch, and smell the exact events of living those lives. Strangely, I sensed no fear or judgments, no guilt, or accountability. I experienced absolutely no blame or shame. I re-experienced every thought, word, and action of all my lives when I focused on them. I became suspended in a sphere of unlimited dimensions.

It is wonderfully liberating to realize there is no guilt, shame, or punishment after death. Although we do take responsibility for our actions, the life review is a learning experience intended to help us realize our reality and our connection to others. It is also one more step in our trek back to our Source. It's intriguing to discover that every time we have contact with another person, ripples caused by our interaction are sent out into the universe and beyond. It doesn't matter what the actions are, they are still wrapped in a giant mantle of love and unconditional acceptance.

People who reported their NDE came away with the realization of the high value of all of life and their connection with it. Some thought that if more people could gain the insights of an NDE, there would be fewer wars and greater cooperation within the world. Others came away feeling that our responsibility is to look after the Earth and its creatures. What a wonderful message to know this deep understanding is coming into the world from beyond.

9

Earth-Like Worlds

Although the environment and nature take a major position for many people, more must be done. Most of us love nature and search for ways to be a part of it. Closeness to nature brings us closer to spirituality. It becomes a place of worship and a way of linking to the mysteries of the universe.

We sit in a quiet place of beauty with feelings of fulfillment and completion. We watch the sun cross the horizon with blazing orange, purple, pink, and blues and long to hold on to that glory forever. We stand on the top of a hill and look across a lush valley or up at the sparkling night sky and wonder at it all. These simple acts are like prayers of love given back to the cosmos as we reach out to become a part of the unknown.

A close connection to nature is a part of the death experience for numerous people who have found themselves in a place unlike anything they have ever seen. There, the plants and living waters sparkled with life and reacted with love and appreciation.

Many NDErs felt the creatures, plants, and water were as much a part of the Oneness as they were themselves. There was a deep feeling of coming home where the colors and music were so magnificent that they struggled to describe the depth of their experience. Here are a few comments from those who returned to tell about their time in heavenly nature.

Derry was in a fatal automobile accident, suffered major head trauma, and went into a coma. While in the coma, she frequently stopped breathing and arrived "*on the other side.*" There, she was joined by Jesus, and together, they floated through a marvelous garden with water that she felt driven to drink.

Everything in the garden had a haze of whiteness and brightness about it. The green of the plants was bright and vibrant. There was an intense glow that surrounded a sparkling stream of water that had a musical sound as it rippled! The water was so dazzlingly clear! I wanted to drink from the stream that ran through the garden where we walked. But when I tried to scoop it up with my hands, it just ran through my hands, yet didn't leave them wet!

It's hard to describe the sensation I felt when the water ran through my hands. It was an overwhelming desire to experience everything about this garden.

One evening **Sarah** was minding her own business while riding her bicycle home from a volunteer position. She had stopped at a red light and was hit from behind by a speeding pickup truck. Unlike most NDEs, Sarah was first startled by demons that enjoyed her shock of their antics. When she realized they were nothing to worry about and couldn't hurt her, they disappeared, and she was left floating in deep blackness. After a short time, a tunnel appeared, and she willingly went through it.

I was in complete darkness. There was no sense of direction or perspective...I looked down at myself and realized that my body was gone. It had been replaced by a pulsing blue-white light cross/star. This seemed quite "natural" and pleasant to me at the time. I felt a strong freeing to no longer be attached to a heavy form.

I flew up the tunnel and glanced in the doorways as I passed. But one that made a lasting impression on me was a world of virtually indescribable beauty. I was looking at a beautiful, wooded garden with fountains, waterfalls, streams, and bridges that glowed and sparkled with shimmering colors. A close representation of the beauty of this world has been depicted by the artist Gilbert Williams, whose work I found several years after my NDE. A sense of peace and harmony flowed from this scene. I moved toward the doorway with a great desire to enter.

Diane was twenty-one and suffered from a tumorous growth in her back. As the mother of a two-year-old boy, she was frightened about her prognosis when she went into the hospital for an operation to remove the growth. She died while the doctors were working on her.

Heaven is real. In fact, it's more real than Earth. The waters sparkle, because they are living waters. And the colors they create are awesome. Everything growing here is also there, but it's far more beautiful and alive. When you concentrate on how beautiful the waters, trees, or the grass are, each responds to the thought with an acknowledgment of love in return. You feel their love towards you for that admiration.

Brian was at a summer picnic when he had a heart attack. By the time the ambulance got him to the hospital, he had flatlined. The hospital tried unsuccessfully to resuscitate him and was forced to pronounce him dead. A sheet was pulled over him, and the morgue was called to take his body. While the hospital did not see any life in his body, the essence that was Brian was very much alive.

I was in an open field. I could feel the breeze blowing and the warmth from the sun. I was able to see thousands of miles in all directions. I saw and sensed every detail of every blade of grass in the field from all around! The grass was bluish green, almost like Turquoise. That's when I saw something running towards me. It was an adorable little Puppy. It was Golden Yellow in color, and I picked it up. It appeared to be so happy to see me! I thought, you look very familiar...Where do I know you from? I've seen you somewhere! He kept licking my hands and tried to lick my face. His tail was wagging, a million times a second.

You might be interested to know that a few days after Brian got home from the hospital, a complete stranger came to the door with the exact same puppy he had seen while dead and gave it to him. The man told Brian a woman had told him that Brian would like the dog. The fascinating part is Brian had never heard of this woman before either.

Dan did not tell the details of what brought about his death. He tells us he did not go through a tunnel. Dan says that he was in his body one moment, and the next, he was standing in a garden. Later, when he woke up in the intensive care unit, he remembered his time there.

I entered the spiritual dimension that I believe was Heaven. It certainly was an afterlife. It was exceptionally beautiful, with gardens and fountains and small countryside hills. The people appeared to be wearing Greek or Roman dress. They seemed very comfortable with white robes and sandal-type shoes. A small group of females were conversing near a majestic water fountain that also exhibited Greek decor, with Seraphim, ivy, and fruit.

I don't recall feeling the wind, sun, or any upper atmosphere or planets. It was just a pleasant and colorful day, yet no weather, sunlight, or water, other than the fountain where the women gathered. It was a very pretty place.

It is hard for us to imagine a garden of beauty and love where water is alive and responsive to our thoughts, like a caring friend. To those of us who have not been through the experience, it may seem like a fantasy. Yet we are repeatedly told of places of nature just like this awaits us when we are finished here. Although the garden is amazingly beautiful and every aspect is astonishingly alive, it only scratches the surface of what awaits us after death.

10

Scared to Death

Most of us love miracles. Just talking about these events causes the hair on our skin to stand at attention. Wonder streaks through us and shoots mystification and yet more questions.

Some people came to NDERF with experiences so close to miracles that they left our heads whirling. Already mentioned in these pages have been numerous miracles of love, power, and new understanding. The stories mentioned in this chapter are of a completely different flavor. The word *miracle* may be debatable from the experiences below. However, they still left those who experienced them shaking their heads in wonder. Dr. Long has called these experiences "fear-death experiences" because they usually happened while the persons involved were in extreme stress and terror.

Jeremy was driving back from boarding school with three other people. The truck ahead had the left turn signal flashing for quite a while, and he thought the driver had forgotten to cancel it. When it had passed places where it could have turned and didn't, Jeremy decided to pass it. Just as he got level with the cab, the truck driver began his turn. Too late, Jeremy realized they were going to be in an accident, and there wasn't a thing he could do to avoid it. That is when something very strange happened.

At this moment, bearing in mind where I was heading and the speed I was going (around 70 to 80 mph), I knew I was going to crash, and my passengers and I were going to die. Although I knew death was certain, I somehow remained remarkably calm, and time almost seemed to stop, as though it was happening in slow motion. The next thing I knew I was in darkness watching a detailed review of my life up to the time of the accident.

Once I absorbed the information, I was told it wasn't my time and that I needed to return. I was hesitant to do that, because I felt such absolute calm, love, and peace that's simply not possible to describe. Without further discussion, I was back in the car, driving along as if nothing had happened and saying to myself that this was impossible. The passengers in the car seemed to be totally unaware of what had happened. It was as if their memories had been erased.

Traci was driving in the mountains with a friend coming home from a camping trip when the front tire blew. They were in the process of going around a bend, and the car immediately went into a crazy skid that convinced Traci this was the end. The only thing to stop them from going over the side of the mountain and down a steep ravine was a guard rail.

I slammed out of my body as I looked at the edge of the mountain that was instant and real. The next thing I knew, I was standing in what appeared to be a circular room with a massive 360^0 movie screen. Time seemed to stop even though my life review seemed like it was only mere seconds.

As quickly as it began, I was blasted back into my body. Time had returned to exactly where I stepped out. Three seconds—two seconds, then the most amazing thing happened. Without any action from me, the car came to a complete stop. I was confused. We had just been skidding on gravel. Somehow it had just stopped. I fell out of the car, barely breathing, on my hands and knees. When I looked, the tires were less than two inches from the edge. Something stopped the car, and it wasn't me.

Unfortunately, there is no further mention of her friend, so we cannot know her reaction to the event.

Brandy was at the beach with friends when she and another girl stood fully dressed at the shore, letting waves roll over their feet. Gradually, Brandy strolled further into the water when a huge wave came at her from nowhere. As she turned to get away, the sand under her feet was scooped out by the wave's undertow, and she fell. The crumbling sand, her wet jeans, and the undertow prevented her escape. She realized she was far out from the shore and didn't think she could get back. Brandy began to wonder why she had to die; she was young and still had not married or had children, and she didn't want to do this to her parents. Here is what Brandy tells us happened next.

It was the most confusing and unbelievable experience yet. I was standing in the water at the shore. My feet had a solid footing on the sand, I looked left at the beach. Although before, the sky had been clear and sunny, it was now a little overcast. The clouds seemed to have a blue, gray, pink, and yellow tint, as though the sun was trying to break through. There was absolutely not a soul on the beach, which was odd since before the beach was packed with people. I felt completely at peace and just wanted to remain there, taking in the beach, sea, and gorgeous sky above me. I heard no voices, as you'd expect.

I remember my last thought while I was in this state was that I wasn't done living; I wanted to do more with my life. At that moment, I clearly decided that I was not going to die. I just wasn't. I didn't want to. Then, suddenly it was sunny, there were people all around me, and my pants were only wet to about mid-calf. I was standing on the beach as a wave—maybe even the one I thought would kill me—splashed around my ankles.

Bo, a young Swedish boy, was known for tempting his luck. One winter, he lived up to that reputation. One day, during school recess, he ran down to the river that ran by the schoolyard property. Bo didn't stop until he was out on the frozen river. The winter was young and only getting a good hold on the land, so the water had not yet frozen through. Bo had gone too far. Out in the middle of the river, the movement of the water under the ice caused it to be too thin, and he fell through. The children with him ran for help while his best friend stayed to try and save him.

My boots and heavy clothes quickly filled with water and began to pull me down under the ice. At that moment, my life started to replay like a movie as I sank deeper and deeper. My friend was holding my hand and trying to pull me out. Then he started to glide towards the ice hole. He could possibly fall into the icy water with me. I told him to let go of me. It was better that only one of us drowned than both of us. At that moment, I had only my head and one arm above the surface of the water. Then, something happened that was beyond all human capacity to understand. Suddenly, we were both lying on firm ice and we could get to the shore. My friend told me later that I suddenly was as light as his younger brother.

Attila was a new young driver in his father's car with a friend. The traffic was heavy, and he was on a two-lane road behind a bus. He was in the process of passing the bus when it started to creep over into the lane his car was in. Attila tells us he was squeezed off the road by the bus and was headed toward a head-on crash with oncoming traffic.

At the moment of impact, I remember a big flash like those old cameras, they used many years ago. Then I saw in black and white like an old film reel flicking through my whole life very fast with little flashes. Somehow I drove from the point of the impact, around a bend, going left and then right, over a train bridge and to the traffic lights at the bottom of the train bridge. I would say that from the point of impact to the lights was two hundred meters. That's when I woke up having no idea what happened to me physically. Mysteriously, we were perfectly parked at the traffic lights, with traffic driving around me. My passanger was terrified and curled up in his seat, pressed against the door, and very white and shaking.

Lynn K Russell

Louis explains that his mother was a rockhound who enjoyed taking his brother, sister, and him with her as she explored the rocks of the nearby mountains. On this particular day, she was investigating a new cave, and Louis climbed to the top of a large hill in search of another opening to the cave from above. That was when he lost his footing and fell thirty to forty feet down a cliff.

I tried to arrest my step but kept sliding. I reached for a branch to stop my fall, but it wads too dry and broke. It made a loud snapping sound when it broke.

At this point, I was falling with my back facing the bottom of the cliff. This is where it gets odd and I'm not offering an explanation—I don't have any. I'm skeptical because I don't know but stay open-minded.

Before my feet left the ground, my knees buckled. Then, my legs pushed out very forcefully, at the last moment. I essentially jumped off the cliff. Except, I am not aware of doing this. It may have been panic, but I did not command my knees to buckle or my legs to push out. Yet, the effect of doing this was that I didn't fall straight down to the cave entrance, where I probably would have been killed instantly by the impact of landing on top of large rocks.

Now, this event gets a bit odder. As soon as my feet left the ground, I was out in space, looking down on the Earth. Immediately, I remember strong emotional distress and loss. Everything I knew as a child was gone—the people, the places, everything. But then again, maybe this was simply a child's natural curiosity. The distress diminished and I was astonished by what I was looking at. The Earth was so beautiful. I remember seeing the large brown areas—the continents—and thinking that the color was wrong. I expected everything to be green, like the mountains where I live, yet so much was brown. Then, I realized that in different climates, not everything was green. The oceans were incredible—so large—covered in clouds everywhere in different shapes.

I turned to look around and saw the stars as you see in the night sky. Yet there were so many more of them. They were so bright and beautiful that for a moment I forgot about the Earth. One of the stars started to become larger and appeared to move toward me. The light from the star was exceptionally bright. I was able to make out a human shape, a staff, and possibly a robe within the light.

I couldn't distinguish any facial features because the light was too bright. I didn't sense that I was seeing at a man or a woman. I had a sense of benevolent intelligence, and gender was irrelevant. There were intense feelings of joy and safety. I knew this new place was safe for a distressed child.

Although I do not recall the details, there was a instant that was like an open book on my life and what my life might be. Then I was told, "You can stay here, or go back."

My first response was emotional. I recalled the distress of everything I had lost and thought, "But I haven't done anything yet."

The instant I thought those words, I opened my eyes, I was laying on the ground, on my back. I was looking up at the thick trunk and limbs of a tall cedar tree and to the blue sky and clouds above. That was also a beautiful sight.

These experiences may leave some people struggling with their own loss. How were the people in these pages spared while we were not? Maybe It's the ones who have gone to the other dimension who are spared, while we are left dealing with life.

We now know those we love who have died are in a place that is far more beautiful, loving, and peaceful than we could ever imagine. We can rest knowing that they are enjoying all those yummy things in the next dimension, and we will be with them one day.

11

Oneness

The overwhelming ecstasy and joy received from being in the Loving Light should have stuffed our emotional bags with enough goodies to last a lifetime, yet we are told there was more. Along with Light and Love, a third element was the complete and inseparable attachment to everything in the universe.

This bond was to the whole cosmos, from the tiniest quantum particle to the enormous universe. And it didn't stop there. They were flabbergasted to realize they were also an intimate aspect of the magnificent Being of Light.

NDErs were astounded to learn that the self they knew as their own being was far greater than they had ever contemplated. As mysterious secrets opened to them, like the petals of a flower, they were wholly connected to the Light and literally *became* the Loving Light.

While the NDErs' full memory of their identity remained, they were miraculously transformed into the Being of Light. They knew—in a way they could not understand—that they had, at a very fundamental level, been intricately involved in the creation of the universe. This awareness was not simply a metaphor but a complete and genuine fact. Additionally, they realized they had taken an active role in the formation of everything that exists everywhere.

They were not simply the acorn that grew a mighty tree; but also, the Earth and water, the sun and rain that helped the tree flourish. They were every molecule in everything, everywhere, and much more. Repeatedly, NDErs realized that the essence of their being, the soul that made them who they were, was the exact same energy as that of the Being of Light. As Rumi said, they were not just a drop from the ocean; they *were* the entire ocean in a drop. And beyond that, they were the Light that created those drops, an intricate, essential part that was impossible to separate.

At death, our perception of the profound essence of our being is realized. In reality, we have never been, nor ever can we be separated from the Oneness.

At this exact moment, while we go on with our daily lives, we are intricately connected to the Creative Force and have been since beyond the beginning of time and space.

This concept isn't new. Throughout history, understanding of our intimate, inseparable connection to the Source has had a place for centuries. Yet, like the preverbal greased pig, it has had difficulty having an enduring hold on our understanding.

Since the 1970s, when Yogananda[13] came to the West and the Beatles visited the ashrams of India, the realization of our Oneness with our fellow humans, all of life, and even our planet has become more and more a part of our conscious Western awareness. Repetitively, those who have been to the Light talk about the harmonious union of all that ever has been—or ever will be. Deep at the root of the Being of Loving Light is a great Oneness.

Some might ask, "How can that be? I'm here and have no idea what the people on the other side of the world are doing

116

at this moment. For that matter, I have no idea what the person across the street is feeling right now. If I were as connected as NDErs imply, would I not be more aware of others around me?"

While in a physical body, we experience a world completely different from the spiritual level. In the hopes of knowing a full human experience, it's important we have individual egos, which help to bring the illusion of separation. Through separation we learn to consciously reach out in love and understanding and experience pain and sorrow. It is not possible to have negative feelings or actions at the spirit level. The lessons of physical existence would not be possible if we retained the awareness of our connection to the Oneness. At that level, the essence of our being is love, and we cannot be otherwise. For us to learn to reach out to one another, and understand all that is available for us here, we need to know existence from an individual perspective.

Another reason we need to experience a sense of separation of a physical body. If we enjoyed the same level of union here as we do after death, our human aspects would be so totally overwhelmed that we would have a difficult time functioning. It would be worse than being in an enclosed area with hundreds of people, and everyone has a radio turned up to top volume and at different stations.

There is one more point to be considered. Although we may have separate experiences, those experiences are shared through humanity. By the time we reach the age of ten, we know what pain, happiness, loss, and success feel like. When we see another person feeling those emotions, we can relate to them and connect through our shared understanding.

As we live our lives day by day, all that we are, do, think, and more is shared with the Source and all the souls that are a part of the Light Being. In that way, Source also learns and grows because no two people see or experience a thing in the same way.

While many people today have accepted the concept of Oneness, it has yet to be taken far enough. Some think of Oneness from the point of view of equality—that we are one in the eyes of God. Others might take it a step further and consider that we are all the same spirit. In that way, we are one, but they fail to extend it to non-living things. Those who have come back tell us that Oneness goes much deeper. They explain that we are indeed much greater than we have ever imagined.

Richard was eight years old when he was hit by a car. He was riding his bike with a friend and, because of a bend in the road, was could not see a car coming as he raced across the street.

The one with a beard told me that I could ask questions and they would answer them, and I would remember what they said. They added that it was important that I do that

First, I asked if we were in heaven.

They explained that it could be if I wanted it to be. They said it could also be hell, if that's what I believed. Reality is an extension of us, instantly realized and formed. We always create our own reality, no matter where we are, for we are all co-creators.

Then I asked them where God was because I couldn't see Him.

They were amused, as if they were giggling at my question. They told me that we can't see something that's part of us. We are all expressions of God. When we see with our eyes, we see through God's eyes. He experiences physical reality through us. When we speak to God, we're speaking to ourselves. We are one and the same with no divisions or separations. We can't see God any more than our hand sees us. It's a part of us and functions because of us and for our purposes, as well as its own. All differences are illusions. The light surrounding us there was God. It was our source of being and was given freely to all."

Next, I asked why this felt this home?

They said that was because it was home. All begins and ends there. It's the starting point for all journeys and lessons."

I don't know why I asked my next question, but it seemed relevant. I asked if, when I returned, I could stay. Their answer was strange.

They doubted I would want to stay very long; I never did. Apparently, I loved the lessons I gained from physical life, especially the hard ones. I was free to choose what I wanted.

Rev. Juliet had colon cancer, and she died.[14] Her occurrence was before Dr. Raymond Moody's book *Life After Life*, so she was feeling very isolated because, so few people understood what she was trying to share with them. I'll let her take you through her episode.

I became aware of a "Being of Light" enveloping me Everything was stunningly beautiful, so vibrant and luminous and so full of life—yes, life! In ways that one would never see or experience on the physical plane.

I was in constant communion with the Light and always aware of its loving presence with me. Consequently, there was no sense of fear whatsoever, and I was never alone. This was a special opportunity to experience being at one with the All— never separate and never at a loss.

The point of this was that we co-create with the Light and are also part of the Light. How fortunate it is to realize that as souls, we are a part of all creation and participate in the actual creative process! Forever and for always, I could never be alone because that's impossible. We are always a part of the Source.

As an aside, Juliet tells us,

I also experienced no blindness (as I do with my physical eyes being legally blind), and what a sense of awe and wonder—to be able to see!

Cara was the typical invincible teenager at the time of her death. At least, that is how she saw herself. She had gone camping with a group of friends. Cara died from an overdose of a concoction of cocaine and other drugs and found an experience she'd never considered.

Suddenly, I no longer had any physical form. Everything was color, lights, music, and patterns, but indescribable. I became part of a communal consciousness, the universe; everything was connected. I felt the true essence of my being. Without form I became a pinpoint of free energy that was connected to thousands of energies of other consciousnesses. All were the perfect balance of the universe. Words don't do justice to illustrate to how it felt to be only energy. A speck of consciousness that's connected to everything in the universe. Time was meaningless; everything was one, and so awe-inspiring. I had no awareness of who I was as a human anymore. Everything was me and I was everything, and it was all connected.

This experience changed Cara's life. It might be of interest to learn that Cara was also legally blind. Yet, during her NDE, she had perfect vision.

It was odd because I had clear vision. I'm legally blind without my glasses. I was able to see in many directions at once. I looked down on my body and out from my body's eyes simultaneously, behind me and outside the tent doors.

Once again, we hear more of **Hafur's** astounding explanation as she tells us of being within the Oneness.

I turned to the light, and swoosh, a telepathic force poured a series of codes filled with millennial wisdom into my mind. Creation, the world, my life, and all other beings that inhabit all the universes. Everything is eternal, spiritual life.

121

Everything belongs to the whole. Any of the distinctions or differences we believe in this life are from ignorance and because we have forgotten this truth.

The light drew me to it like a giant magnet. I was immersed within its interior, where all that existed was light. I forgot I my body and became fused with the light. In that instant, I experienced a feeling of plural unity and understood everything with extreme clarity.

From my heart sprang a great aha! Like a co-participant of creation.

We live in Plural Unity or Oneness. Our reality is Unity in Plurality and Plurality in Unity. We are everything, and everything is us, without essential differences other than temporal appearances.

God is everything, and everything is God, just as life itself.

Consciously living with love for all creation is the essence of life itself. Love is made manifest and materializes in this level of existence as a cohesive force to recreate itself in multiple forms. It's a game in which nothingness recreates itself in temporal, illusory events.

I understood that what we call God is the silence of indescribable life of everything and in which everything exists or is within it—a marvelous, loving, and conscious eternity. The perpetual creation of consciousness.

Wayne died when another car slammed into him while pushing a disabled vehicle. Here, he shares the knowledge he gained while dead. He says that he was raised as a Southern

Baptist. His experience was quite different from what he expected based on what he had been taught.

I became aware of what appeared to be a flowing silver river that shimmered as it flowed. Each drop in the river was a different color, yet everything flowed together as one body of apparent liquid. Nothing made me think that this was actually water or a river, that is just the best descriptive example that I can give of something for which there are no words. The main body of the flow was silvery shimmering lights seemed to be composed of different colored drops within the flow. I understood that these droplets were the experiences of all who had lived.

Although these experiences existed as separate items, yet they belonged to the whole. They were the collective knowledge of all. I understood there were no individuals, just one, although each experience individually was the whole. This concept of One is so foreign to any explanation I can give. There is simply no other way of describing it. Previously, my understanding of one was a single uniqueness. In this case, One was something else. Many being One and One being many, all existing simultaneously in the same time and space.

Further, I understood that these collective experiences were omniscient knowledge—everything ever spoken, heard, and experienced. Those colored drops contained infinitely detailed experiences, right down to the memory of every cell division and every thought. All experiences were known instantly by the collective consciousness that was the stream. Every experience could be comprehended at though it was a first-person experience happening at the time it originally occurred.

Lou was a young soldier celebrating his last night in the Navy. He had no thought of God or spirit as he sped down the road to the party being given in his honor. That was when he was in a serious car accident and died. While having an NDE, the Light told him of his Oneness. When he didn't understand, the following is what he experienced as a way of explaining this concept.

The Light said all that existed was of me, who are of me. But these will come to me, and I will care for them more. They will fly apart and come back together at the time of the Gathering. I wondered if he was saying these were my children. But I was only twenty-one and not married, nor planned to be. I couldn't understand how all this was of me and me of Him. Then, a stunning crystal serving platter appeared, shimmering in the colors of many rainbows. In an instant, it shattered into thousands of pieces and splinters. Yet, each one had its own brilliance. Then, ever so slowly, it began to come back together to form the original serving platter. Now I understood what this Being of Light was showing me; we are the pieces of the platter. I was one of the thousands of bits, as was all those there and those back in the world. All those pieces would eventually return to God.

Our enmeshment with the Light and the reality of our being is a deep and meaningful part of all that is. It's like looking into space and seeing a great wholeness, yet when we look very closely, we see that it's made up of gazillions of particles. The more aware we are of our connectedness to the One and each other, the more we are compelled to bring greater goodness to the world.

Thich Nhat Hanh, a well-known Buddhist monk, explains his view of Oneness:[15]

"Feelings, whether of compassion or irritation, should be welcomed, recognized, and treated on an absolutely equal basis, because both are us. The tangerine I am eating is me. The mustard greens I am planting are me. I plant with all my heart and mind. I clean this teapot with the kind of attention I would have were I giving the Buddha or Jesus a bath. Nothing should be treated more carefully than anything else. In mindfulness, compassion, irritation, mustard green plant, and teapot are all sacred."

How fantastic to have the opportunity to learn from the amazing experiences NDErs have shared with us. Their accounts offer a deeper realization of the spiritual world and our reality. At a spiritual level, we are the flour in bread, so intricately enmeshed with the whole that we are indistinguishable from All. Our task is to realize this intricate connection with one another and reach out in love and respect for our differences, no matter what religion, race, color, or size. No matter what people do for a living, no matter whether they are locked in a jail cell, each is an expression of the One, and that's it; there's nothing more. There is a new word that exemplifies this concept: Nonduality.

Paramahamsa Yogananda, a spiritual leader of the Beatles, once said, *"I have lived through all of you."* He realized his Oneness with the Source and through this Oneness with each of us. Richard Bach talks about Oneness in his books *Illusions* and *One*. Deepak Chopra said, *"We are not in the world, but the world is in us."* Anthony De Mello, a Catholic priest from India and teacher of our spiritual Oneness; Joel Goldsmith; and Eckhart Tolle, a German-born, Canadian author and speaker on spirituality; Gangaji, a female American guru of spirituality and Oneness; Adyashanti, an

American guru; Ken Wilber[16] and Lynne McTaggart[17] are only a few of the well-known spiritual people today who share the same message being brought back by our NDE friends.

We have a part in the creation of every neutrino, photon, atom, and cell in the universe, as the NDE reports tell us. That concept is humbling and may be difficult to integrate into our philosophy as we battle against centuries of confused information passed down from generation to generation.

Life is a fantastic game the soul plays. Human development, all sciences, and every one of the numerous discoveries that have been, or ever will be, are simply a part of the game. During our time here in the physical dimension, we develop personalities and ways to view life and the world around us. Over time, our attachment to this personality takes steel-like strength as we immerse ourselves in the ego we created. We believe the ego *is* our reality; it is who and what we are. Now, we are discovering a new truth.

Most of us are aware of another aspect of us that we call "soul." We see that element existing out there somewhere in the illusive ether. From that perspective, our souls are aware of what we do, like an exalted oversoul that has a small connection with us. Then, it takes over at the moment of our death and goes on to the afterlife.

It's important to realize that we are soul right now, right here, today. We may think we have a personality, the ego that is us. In reality, we are soul, period. It's our souls that are living this life and only soul, nothing else.

One final point before we leave Oneness. There are no races. These differences are just a part of the illusion. The perceived differences in our world between people are the delicious spices added to an elaborate feast. They are different styles of fashion and are there for our pleasure.

12

Time

Einstein's Theory of Special Relativity tells us time and space are not only entangled as spacetime, but he also states they are illusions. Astrophysicists explain that spacetime began simultaneously with the Big Bang, as if it were a part of the package. Both time and space are so completely interwoven into our lives, not only is it difficult for us to imagine operating without them, but it's their existence that makes life possible for us.

Recently, scientists have come to the realization the universe operates much like a giant two-dimensional hologram; in fact, there are several who say it *is* a hologram. David Bohm was a highly respected physicist who worked with quantum physics during World War II until he died in 1992. He was best known for his work on the holographic model of the universe. In his book *The Holographic Universe*, Michael Talbot explains David Bohm's discovery of the holographic nature of the universe and the importance that the illusion of time and space plays in our physical life.[18] Talbot tells us,

"In a holographic universe, even time and space could no longer be viewed as fundamentals. Because concepts such as location break down in a universe in which nothing is truly separate from anything else, time and three-dimensional space, like the images of a fish on the TV monitors, would also

have to be viewed as projections of this deeper order. At its deeper level, reality is a super-hologram in which the past, present, and future exist simultaneously."

(In reference to the fish, Michael Talbot uses an example in his book of two television monitors showing an image of the same fish from altered angles. To outside observers watching the two screens, it appears that they are seeing two different fish.)

Talbot takes the concept of the holographic nature of the universe and expands his theories of how ESP, psychic phenomena, and the supernatural could be based in reality. I support Talbot's position on psychic phenomenon. Through oneness, mentioned in the last chapter, it makes sense that we could be in touch with these abilities.

It's interesting to note that those who experienced an NDE also found that time and space had become nothing more than the sleight of the magician's hand. It's like something you see from the corner of your eye, but when you turn your head for a better look, nothing is there.

Time and space are essential ingredients for physical matter to exist. There would be no universe without them. But at the spirit level, physical is nonexistent, and spacetime is unnecessary.

To offer you, the reader, a more complete understanding of this part of the NDE, I turned to the people on the chat forum at NDERF for their thoughts on time and space. Such marvelous answers were shared. These are only a couple of them.

Modern quantum physics agrees with Einstein that the spacetime continuum is an illusion. This property can be present where physical matter exists. Here is Azure's wonderful explanation,

"In a universe, where there is no matter and no particles, there is no time either. In such universes, the linear time going from past, surpassing present, and heading to future itself would collapse into a singular moment, Kairos, where past, present, and future simultaneously exist. Such "omni-time" or "being-time" would be immensely flexible, and you would not be able to distinguish between a second and a month. Traveling back in time in such kairos would be possible."

Based on Azure's explanation, without time, everything that ever was or ever will be is happening right now, simultaneously. In that case, if we could capture that element here in the physical, we could instantly see into the past, present, or future and participate in any of those time zones at our leisure.

A similar concept is explored in the next comment. This fascinating bit came from one of the moderators, Dave T., as he talked about Anita Moorjani's amazing experience. He tells us,

"In her experience, she went back in "time" during her NDE...and "removed" the energy that manifested in her body as cancer. This act then had consequences in current "time" as her body adjusted in time to that removal, and within a very short span of "time" no cancer was located. Changing the past, as seen in her experience, has an influence on the present...and the future. Her experience seems to point to an ability to transcend the effect of time to alter it or change the

effect of choice and to point to the awareness of being able t *touch "emotions."*

[It is important to note here that this is Dave's concept o what happened for Anita Moorjani, and may not fit he expectation in her book, *Dying to be Me.*]

As amazing as it seems, we are talking about an actual *documented* experience, not a science fiction story—the stuf of miracles. We will be hearing directly from Anita Moorjan later in this book.

Those who died returned with the full acceptance that, i the other dimension, time does not exist and is the physica existence's special domain. Indeed, some NDErs came bacl to tell us that while they were on the other side, everythin was happening simultaneously.

Let us take a moment to look at some of the othe comments about time.

Denise died during the birth of her third child Apparently, she was given laughing gas to administer t herself as needed through the night and gave herself more thar was acceptable. She almost killed her baby along with herself

I had the opportunity to view the universe and be one witl *it. While at the same time, I had full understanding of the trutl* *of existence. It went into things such as time is simultaneous,* *thus, everything happens at the same time. There is no past,* *present, or future.*

Cynthia had worked around jet exhaust and fuel for several years, and she tells us her lungs were a mess. She had asthma and a yearly bout of pneumonia requiring hospitalization, so her lungs were quite badly scarred. As a result, she had trained her child that if she was having problems breathing, she would give a signal, and the child would know to call 911. This is what happened one day only Cynthia did die and had an amazing experience.

When I arrived at the energy source, the universe was instantly created right in front of me. I saw everything that happened since the beginning of the Big Bang, like on the Discovery Channel. Time is an illusion; there is no such thing as time. It's all simply a series of events. It seemed like a big paisley of the cosmos being formed before me, and I had Superman's vision. I existed beyond the far reaches of the universe and beyond the universe, seeing everything with super-vision. I could see Earth, my house, and everything inside it. And it was all from a bazillion gazillion light years past the edge of the universe.

Cynthia's experience in our time lasted only about fifteen minutes, Yet, in the other dimension, it was as if she'd been there for an eternity.

Bryan died in a way that is one of my biggest nightmares. He was fooling around with some university friends when he accidentally fell over an upper railing and down a stairwell to the stairs below. At the time of the accident, Bryan was a philosophy major and had become cynical of his Christian

133

upbringing. During his death experience, he saw everything from a completely different perspective.

I saw the reality of our world in real human time. Yet, I also relived the entirety of my life in an intermingled way.

The linear span of my life intensified into one brilliant point that could exist transcendent of time. My traditional notion of time was being shattered. In fact, that concept no longer made any sense because I realized that all moments occurred simultaneously.

Mark was a teenager who lived in the southern mountainous part of America. On the day of his death, there was a sudden snowstorm, severe enough that he was hoping for a day off school. No such luck. Although he made it to school, later that day, he was in a vehicle that ran into a telephone pole. His report of the experience is quite extensive, yet only after he was asked if he had any sense of altered space or time, did he explain.

All points in time exist simultaneously. In a sense, there is no time. Time is meaningless. I had a perception of a place where time did exist. But for the moments outside, in the place with the other, there was no time.

James had two NDEs and a close call. His first NDE was when he was four, and he drowned. The next one was as a teen when he overdid the magic mushrooms. His close call was during a heart attack as an adult. During his second death, he shared the following observations about time and space.

It was revealed that I was not in normal space/time; I was somehow outside of it. Yet I could observe and experience things simultaneously at differing levels of space and time.

I had stepped out of normal space and time. Thus, even an experience that involve a great deal of time, could occur in a fraction of a second.

Jerome had a heart attack but refused to seek help because he had an important project he wanted to complete. One of the questions NDERF asked him of his NDE was, "Did you become aware of future events?" Jerome said no and went on to tell us,

Contrarily to normal human perception, I had a intense sense of "now-ness." There was no time to divide into past, present, or future. What would (or might) happen was closely linked to the "now" of what was happening. It seemed to be an integral part of now rather than as divided time.

The concept of no time and space at the spirit level is intriguing and leaves questions stacked to the ceiling like books in a library. Is it possible one of the reasons we are here in the physical world is to experience time and space? Hypothetically, could we leave this life, live a completely different lifetime as another person, and then return to this life moments after we die to complete this one? In the chapter, Are

They Really Dead, Jack tells us that is exactly what happened to him. Pretty fantastic—and yet, with no time or space, we should be able to die in the twenty-first century and reincarnate into another life at any point in the past or future—and perhaps we do. The possibilities are both mind-boggling and enticing.

While the concept is appealing, there is one major catch: time and space may only exist physically, but so do we. For us to take advantage of this phenomenon, it would be necessary to step out of this level of existence and enter into another dimension. But don't rush it; there is plenty of time.

13

Suicide

The topic of suicide is reported in this book with the understanding that it is a part of the near-death experience that needs to be examined. However, I want to stress that I do not condone or suggest anyone choose that direction.

The mere thought of suicide sends shivers of revulsion down the spine like a bitter, cold wind to the senses. We empathize with those left behind and feel frustrated in our uselessness to take away their sorrow. Suicide is the most painful type of loss there is. It dumps a load of guilt, anger, and confusion onto those left behind. Understandably many churches warn that suicide is a sinful act and erroneously promise dreadful punishment on the other side.

It is interesting to learn those who return from killing themselves report no shame or punishment was doled out because of their actions. Like tasting chocolate for the first time, they tell of being fully engulfed in unconditional love, peace, and joy beyond description. However, it's important to note that many explained they were clearly told suicide was not their choice to make.

An online article called, I don't want to live, but I don't want to die, published by American Mental Health, tells us that the majority of people who commit suicide don't want to die. They just want to stop their anguish. They are seeking oblivion. Imagine how surprised they are to find themselves still existing after death.

Those who returned said they were given three choices. They could remain in the other dimension with the understanding they would be required to return to the physical realm to live a new life with all the same elements as the one they were trying to escape. They would then be required to face the situations with the understanding they had to work out their issues without choosing death as a solution.

Another choice was to return to their present lives and work their issues through without killing themselves. The final choice was to stay in that dimension and as though caught in the repetitive spiral of a science fiction movie, they were to go over and over the conditions that pushed them to kill themselves by entering what I call a spiritual loop. They had to repetitively relive the situation that brought them to suicide until they came to a solution that did not include bringing about their own death.

Clearly, the bottom line in these choices is suicidal people need to face the situations that pushed them to take their lives and work them through to a different option. Undoubtedly, we are the ones who choose the life circumstances they are now living. Those conditions were to help with their spiritual learning and growth. There is no escape through death because, in reality, there is no death.

With respect to those presented in this chapter, I have chosen not to use names or add identifying information in these reports except for one. Debi-Sue Weiler has asked to be identified, and a link to her book has been added to the notes.[19]

The first account we will look at was from an alcoholic man who was depressed at the direction his life was taking and chose suicide. Here, we open his story while he's on the other side with a guide at his side.

My guide and I were floating above a pit of some sort that contained a very depressing scene. The landscape was devoid of beauty or life. The people there shuffled around, their heads down and their shoulders hunched forward in a depressed, resigned manner. As they wandered here and there, looking at their feet, they occasionally bumped into one another, but they kept on going. It was horrible to think that I was going to be cast down with these confused, lost souls. The voice understood my terror and eased it by telling me that this is a Hell of my own creation. Eventually, you would have to go back to Earth and experience a new life all over again, while faced with the same difficulties that you faced in this lifetime. You will stay here, with these lost and confused souls until then. Suicide isn't an escape. You cannot do with your life whatever you please. Nor can you choose death."

I was speechless. My brain couldn't think. I sobbed even harder. The voice-presence must be the Holy Spirit sent to me, I thought. Softer, the voice continued, "I'm not finished with you; your work isn't complete. Return and do what you were meant to do.

Interestingly, this man saw a landscape devoid of life and beauty, while those who went to the garden after a normal death could not stop talking about the beauty.

There are several reports of a place NDErs have witnessed where people shuffle around, lost in their own personal anguish, similar to Hafur, who saw her grandfather in the tunnel. Perhaps these souls chose to stay in the other dimension and work out a different solution. In most of their accounts, these souls were accompanied by a spirit guide there to help them, yet we are told the lost ones were oblivious to the angelic presence.

This next account is scary enough to turn anyone away from suicide. This woman felt very depressed and alone. All hope of a better future seemed gone. She took an overdose of potent sleeping pills. Instead of the oblivion she was reaching for, she found she was very much alive.

When I awoke, I was immersed in deep blackness. I tried to see my hand but couldn't. Nothingness surrounded me. Then, I slowly began to hear noises. Bit by bit they gradually became louder until I realized what I was hearing. It was the moaning and groaning of what sounded like hundreds (maybe even thousands) of people shouting, screaming, and crying in pain and sorrow. I couldn't see them. All I could do was listen to their anguish. Fear overtook my heart and panic settled in. Then I felt a sensation of something crawling up my legs. First the left and then the right. Instinctively, I knew that if whatever it was, engulfed me, then I would be caught in this place forever. Then, I would be one more of those who were left in their agony. As the sensation came neared my belly, I saw this large, bright hand reach in. I could see the light of this hand. And I heard that soft and authoritative voice say, "My child, this is not what I want for you!"

This young man was adopted and felt unwanted and sorry for himself. He particularly felt alone when his parents went on a trip, and he was left at home with his grandfather. That is when he took an overdose of pills and anything else he could find in the medicine cabinet.

I knew my eyes were open there in the room. That's when I felt the pulling...I tried to see myself, but every time I looked down, all I saw was nothing but the blackness of the tunnel wall. The fear was like nothing ever I want to feel again. Then, I was moving faster. My vision turned and I tried to see my bedroom. But now it was like a flashlight shining in the dark about a mile away. As before, the fear was overwhelming.

It was about then that I realized that if I look toward where I was headed, I'd be lost...

By the way, I learned a lot of things very quickly. The terrible thing I became aware of was that hell is being cut off from life. You know you were—something—but you can't remember what that is, and there is more, but you can't remember what the means. It's right there, on the tip of your tongue. Wait, what's a tongue? What am I again? Over and over, hell is trying to sink your teeth into this mystery with no success. Just as you think you got it—nothing is there.

That voice came again. It sounded so calm and told me it's not my time to choose death. Life is a gift. I had been selfish. My mind was filled with so many things. When I saw the light from my room like a far-off star, I felt so ashamed and naked to everything.

The message this man shared about the events was profound. They teach lessons about many things we do not like in our lives.

I was severely depressed and overdose. A neighbor found me about four hours later. I floated above the ambulance and watched the paramedics cut off my clothes. Next, I was going through a dark brown/green cloudy/smoky tunnel. Then, I was at a place that I can only describe as being outside. I saw the entire universe, galaxies, stars, planets, and the Earth. My perceptions were confused. While I had an overwhelming sense of all-Oneness, it was accompanied by a feeling of wrong. I was absolutely alone, without the presence of God. I sensed something behind me or knew something was there. Somehow, I felt that if I turned and looked, I would be there forever. That was not a comforting place. Then, I saw the universe being destroyed before my eyes. It all turned from brown to fire from right to left, starting with the Earth. It was my personal universe that was being destroyed, not anyone else's. The destruction of mine would have no effect on anyone else.

This fellow drowned himself during a time of depression. He does not tell us much about what led up to his actions, but the learning he gained is enlightening.

I didn't feel myself leave my body. It seemed to just fall away. I felt I had lost a friend. There was a terrible feeling of loss, and I knew I was dead. But I was still aware! I thought I should be seeing a tunnel and a light. I was like a thought in space, utterly alone in nothingness. I waited and waited some more. Then, I realized what I'd just done.

Will I be here in this abysmal place forever? What have I done! My fear was off the charts. We aren't supposed to take our own life. I was fully conscious of what I'd done. The thought of being alone in nothing forever was unbearable. But what could I do? It was too late.

Suddenly, within the void, I heard a voice. It told me not to worry, everything is fine and it would work out perfectly. I went from overwhelming terror to total peace and acceptance of my life and my responsibility. I no longer worried about heaven or hell or even my death. This voice had accepted me and didn't judge me. In a way, had already evaluated myself and had an instant understanding of my life and how important it is to play our lives out to the end, regardless of how hard it is. I needed to get off myself and be in the company of others to help each other. That abyss was infinite separation from all. I was in the I AM.

Not all NDEs brought about by suicide are negative. Some people return after having very positive experiences, yet their messages are the same, and they will never try suicide again.

This woman had been severely depressed for some time after giving birth. Although we are not told specific details of what led to her suicide, she does say she just wanted to end the pain with pills.

I overdosed on pills. I just wanted to end the pain. I told the children goodbye and got into a hot tub of water.

*I felt a shock. I was in a blue, misty expanse and detecte
and then saw some beings. Three figures seemed to be waitin
for me. I spoke with them. They wanted me to decide if I wa
done with my life's task. Parts of my life race through my min
and saw I wasn't meeting my goals. They explained that I ha
picked this life as a test. I needed to choose to return to m
body or reincarnate. But the goal would still be the same.*

Here, we have a child of eleven who was not eve
thinking of suicide until she listened to the lyrics of a song
The lyrics made her think of all the things wrong in her life
and she was stabbed herself. It's amazing that this child had
knife there ready to do the job.

*I picked up the knife under my bed to kill myself. Suddenl
a white light appeared and a girl about sixteen or seventee
walked out. She came up to me and wrapped her arms aroun
my shoulders. She told me everything was going to be alrigh
I was so scared. I kept asking her who she was. She just sai
that it didn't matter and that she was my comforter.*

[Later, she met a man who talked to her.] *The man tol
me to correct the things wrong in my life. Fix all the thing
that were your fault. Just admit that you did wrong. But don
remind others of what they did wrong. I felt confused. I sai
that I didn't want to go back. I knew what I had done wa
wrong and needed to fix things, but it felt so peaceful there.
never want to go back there! I belonged here from now an
forever.*

*The girl told me that I didn't realize what was going on
They were sending me back so that I could fix my life and star*

off anew. They are trying to give me the life I had always wanted." I pleaded with them to not leave me alone. I wanted them with me. The girl told me that she would come and visit sometimes and then we could talk to each other. I said that was good and I would be willing to go back to my body.

Debi-Sue is the one exception to my rule about identifying a person who tried suicide. She is one more person who committed suicide by overdosing but doesn't elaborate on her reasons for wanting to be dead, except to say she was depressed and fed up with life and humanity. She explains she was very aware killing herself was wrong but, by that time, she simply didn't care. She was in pain and wanted the peace of oblivion. She had lost all hope her life would ever get better and was aware that what she was doing would cause her death; it was not an accident. She wrote the obligatory suicide note, lay down on the couch, and reached out for death. She was trying to get away from one life only to end up still very much alive in another.

I got dizzy right away and the hallucinations began. Friends emerged from nowhere to talk me out of killing myself. I slumped over to one side on the couch. I was surprised to chat with friends that I hadn't seen in years. They sat in the easy chair beside the sofa or paced up and down in front of me as they talked. They were as real as you and I. But I resisted their efforts. I knew they weren't there. They were just projections of my mind.

145

DW says this of her actual passing,

There was a sense or an awareness, of something like a tiny "click." Like a cork pulled from a bottle, a release like the tension released from a spring as I died. Then, I knew I was dead.

There was quiet; Complete silence—no apartment noises, no neighbor noises, no traffic noises, and no body noises— nothing. I liked it. So peaceful. Darkness was all around me. Yet, even in that darkness, I felt the complete peace of the silence. It confused me that I was still conscious.

What I'm trying to share with each person is, I think my experience might help others. That is the main point of sharing my story.

I didn't die. You will not die.

My body was dead. I was still very much alive. I knew it then and I know it now as truth.

My body had stopped working. The self I am, did not.

I tried to understand what was happening to me; I was still me. I was apparently alive. I couldn't see myself. I could not raise my hand and look at it. But I was something, I still felt like myself.

At this point, Debi-Sue traveled to the Light and had a magnificent experience we discussed in chapter 15 on Love. For those who would like to look up Debi-Sue's NDE, she is recorded on the NDERF website under the name DW.

Although some of these experiences seem tempting, others jump out as a repellent gamble. It's interesting to learn research done by Dr. Bruce Greyson[20] has shown even those who have had the most positive experiences will never try to kill themselves again. Suicide might alleviate the immediate pain of the one who has died, but it stands mountain high as the cruelest way to leave this world for those left behind. Those people are left running in circles with guilt, shame, and confusion. They are left asking endless questions about why their loved one felt it best to take that course of action and what they could have done differently to stop it from happening. For this reason, anyone contemplating suicide should consider that time moves on, the sun continues to come up every morning, and as the medieval Sufi poet said, "This too shall pass."

14

Hell and Evil

For many, Hell has taken on a strong presence. It has become identified with a powerful, diabolical entity standing in the wings of life, greedily waiting to take over the human soul. It is endowed with such supremacy it's above the angels and sits with the highest spiritual deities of influence. When this demonic beast isn't busy torturing and deceiving pathetic, unsuspecting humans, it spends its time honing new, ghastly skills to use against us. Then, this monster may be seen as an insidious undercurrent that takes over people's lives and rules like a malicious puppeteer.

Today, most people realize we can decide how much authority we want to give this illusion. We have enough information to make up our minds about the reality of an entity waiting to pounce at the first opportunity to take over our lives, kidnap our senses, and control our behavior. We finally enjoy the freedom of taking full responsibility for our actions without concern over a leering diabolical entity interfering. We know that no matter how robustly we envision an overpowering evil entity, our claims do not make it so.

Throughout history, many great thinkers have understood the true nature of evil. Yet, it's only since the Industrial Revolution that the general population has been set free to discover new ways of knowing. We now stretch our minds throughout the universe in a quest for answers to our never-ending questions. In the process, the dark glasses have fallen off, and we see a new reality like a polished gem.

Goodness and evil have existed as fraternal twins since we first populated the world. The experiences of our NDE friends reveal that we are here to learn lessons of the spirit, and our dual nature remains as long as humans need both sides as learning tools.

There is no evil entity to attach the blame for our actions and the world's woes upon. We can search under the bodies sprawled on the ground or scour in the deepest pits of bombed-out destruction and find nothing more than our own choices gaping back at us. No matter how hard we work to divert the blame, we can no longer peg the liability on that old convenient scapegoat. The Devil is dead, and we are left with our own choices and actions staring back at us.

The awareness of a negative entity dates back over 3,500 years to the time of Mesopotamia,[21] when the belief in many gods dominated the world of the spirit. Around that time, a man named Zoroaster strolled into the world of mythology's numerous deities with a theory that there were only two gods. One god, Ahura Mazdah, he explained, was the good god and the other, Angra Mainyu, lied. It was up to people to choose the good god and avoid the lying god. It should be stressed here that Zoroaster never saw the lying god as evil; it was simply a fact of life, like liquid flowing downstream. Basically, the age-old question of good and evil.

Many people of Zoroaster's time really liked his theory and took to it like a thirsty man to water. Over time, it became quite popular as fingers of the idea spread from Turkey around the end of the Mediterranean Sea to Judea and Israel. The Jews didn't accept more than one God, nor could they agree that God could have a negative nature. It is not until the book of Job in the Old Testament of the Bible that we find the first mention of Satan. This being was not considered evil as he challenged God to put Job to a test. The word *Satan* in Hebrew means "the accuser."

The concept of hell gradually took shape. On the North side of the Mediterranean Sea, people believed that after death, the soul was picked up by a boatman and taken to the land of Hades. There was little understanding of what that was except that it was under the Earth.

Around that same time, the Jews wisely got rid of their garbage by burning it in a dump just outside their cities. But trash was not the only thing that got incinerated. That same blazing dump was also where they got rid of their criminals. On the day of the burning, they dragged their criminals over to the dump and threw them into the burning refuse. Eventually, this image of burning souls together with Hades underground became a representation of hell.

Once more, no concept of an evil entity existed, although there was a strong concept of wrongdoing and punishment. The perception of evil didn't come until later when a new name was added to Satan, and he became the Devil. Then, like a chemistry student working in a lab, various elements of evil were added to the concoction. Over the last two thousand years, the concept of an evil creature has grown to the point that it encompasses approximately seventy-five names for the being originally known as Satan. And each one of these names relates to the same thing: evil.[22]

Humans are the only Earthly creatures to have thoughts of death and evil. Nowhere in the animal kingdom is there a sense of evil or sin nor the concept of death. There, things are simply what they are. It appears that the development of evil was related to our fear of death coupled with our curiosity and creative ability.

Throughout human existence, we have demonstrated a wonderful ability to create, starting with the primitive tools held by furry creatures destined to be our ancestors. Today, our creativity shows itself in amazing architecture, transportation, and countless inventions, along with art, music, dance, writing, and remarkable philosophical and scientific concepts. Indeed, it is provocative and intriguing to realize humans are the only evil in the world.

Not many near-death experiences fit into the hellish category. That may be because those experiences took people into regions that would terrify the Devil himself. Perhaps those NDErs who found themselves in a demonic setting did not want to disclose what they saw as their badness and add further ejection to their list of concerns. Then again, it may simply be that few people have frightening NDEs.

We are told that frightening experiences derive from people's feelings of what they deserve. The view that unpleasant experiences stem from those having the event is punctuated by their wide variety. Positive NDEs also vary, but like a knit sweater, they have a pattern. Not so with negative experiences. As you will see from the reports shared here, none are similar or have the same elements, except that they were in a downward direction and encompassed horror.

Because of the sensitive nature of this subject matter, and with consideration to the individuals who experienced these negative NDEs, I have not included any personal information that would identify them or link to their reports.

(1) *Suddenly, I plunged downward, almost like being sucked into a vortex. Total blackness. There was absolutely no light. Eventually, I saw a distant light and was curious about it. I sensed myself being moved steadily toward the light. Until I was approximately thirty to fifty feet away, then, I noticed the light give the impression of flames coming from inside a doorway. A dark, ominous figure stood to the right of the outer door frame. It was clear that he was evil. His hand kept beckoning me inward in kind of a rolling hand motion. I became terrified. Sounds like soul-wrenching screams, not of pain but screams of the soul, emitted from the fire behind him. Although I tried to pull back, I discovered I could not.*

On both sides of me, guides appeared. Their job was to provide guidance and the energy to keep me moving forward. I kept trying to pull back but discovered it wasn't possible, as I had no physical form. Thus, nothing to pull back with. It felt like a huge magnet was steadily dragging me into the fire. I started screaming to Let me Die. I knew I was crying about the impossible because I wanted my soul to die. Repeatedly, I screamed out to let me die. That was preferable to entering the doorway.

(2) *Suddenly, an angel appeared. He was wearing combat vestments like a soldier. He stood about five meters high. I asked him who he was. He replied, "Do you care? I am Michael, and I'm here to take you to another place. It felt like I was being suctioned downward. I arrived at a lake of blood and rotten, burnt flesh. The smell of rotting flesh was unbearable.*

Holes opened in the ground at each step I made, and horrible worms appeared. I looked up and saw a man bending down while a beast raped him. The demon had the head of a donkey. On the right, was the anus of a gigantic, defecating demon. On the left, were people dancing. They wanted to stop, but the demons wouldn't let them. The demons saw me and tried to attack, but Michael made the symbol of the cross, and the demons backed away swearing against God, Michael, and myself. Michael hugged me and took me out of there. Then he told me that I was to make a choice. That this was my last chance. I had seen both paradise and hell and it was up to me from now on. I returned to my body and recovered.

(3) A form came toward me that was neither male nor female, young or old, alive or dead. It was mocking me when it laughed.

Anger flooded through me, while, at the same time, I was overwhelmed with a strong sexual desire for this being. It thought this was very funny. "You fucking bitch!" It came nearer. I started to caress it and kiss it. I felt drunk and even more out of control. My mind kept telling me this was so wrong. Everything I'd been taught to live in goodness and right was not making any sense. When I looked at the being, I was extremely terrified! The strong sexual desire was taking control even though I knew everything was wrong about this "creature." Wrong age (it seemed to be a young child), wrong sex (I'm heterosexual), and wrong morality (it exuded evil).

(4) My eyes opened, and I was in a certain chamber of hell. Putrid smells assaulted me. The darkness was so deep, one could feel it. People were in chains and being tortured in such horrendous, ghastly ways, that I still cannot talk about them. I hated that place, and desperately wanted to leave, but

could not. I was stuck there watching, smelling, and feeling all the pain and horror of that place.

(5) This next person had a negative experience while going through the life review segment of her NDE. That fact seems significant to what this individual thought she deserved.

During the life review, an evil being was there. Surprisingly he was handsome not ugly as I would expect. He had black hair, medium build, and dressed in a black robe with a black cord at the waist. His eyes grabbed my attention. They were a complete void! There was **no** *life nor goodness in them. His primary purpose was to possess, own, and control my Soul. I shrank back in horror. Every time I erred or failed, he clearly enjoyed it immensely and shouted, "There! Look at how she messed up? Why didn't she do a better job or help more? She should be punished." I was desolate. My poor small and limited good works couldn't measure up to God's perfect standard. I believed I deserved anything I got.*

(6) *It wasn't that I could see the blackness; it just existed, and I knew it was there. Abruptly, there were strange beings all around me. I don't remember how many, but I sensed that they had been around me for a while just waiting for this moment. They began to pull at me and took me to a place of absolute, total desperation.*

Clearly, none of these reports are like the others except that they talk about the ugliness of those having the experience envisioned as hell.

Sadly, some returned to life before the next stage in these events. Although I'm unsure what the criteria are for this to happen, frequently, these souls were eventually taken out of their nightmare existence and brought to heaven.

Repeatedly, when the individual was pulled out of hell, they asked what had happened. Each time, they were told that it was of their own making, that they were the ones who created that experience because they thought that was what they deserved.

Several people were directly told there was no such thing as sin or evil. For everyone who had a hell experience, there was an equal number who supported the theory that evil and sin did not exist.

(A) *The truth is that there is no such thing as evil. There is no such thing as sin, nor is there any such thing as hell. The only hell is the one we create ourselves through our fearful and ignorant minds.*

(B) *All I ever heard or knew was swept away. I realized that Christ had not died on the cross for our sins. I understood there was no sin or evil. I had a certainty that I'd existed since the moment of creation and would always exist. And that all consciousness is perpetually in the act of becoming. I realized that we have freewill and that we choose everything.*

(C) *God is absolute love. Unconditional Love cannot have any relationship with evil, the devil, hell, purgatory, sin, karma, retribution, or any judgment, blame, and retribution.*

(D) *The first doorway I peeked into resembled a classic idea of hell. I wanted to leave, so there was no difficulty doing so. My feeling was that anyone could quit hell if they wanted. I sensed that no one or nothing had put those people in captivity except their personal belief in the agony they continued to suffer.*

There is yet one more aspect of evil to be considered. As long as we exist in this physical body, adversity will be a part of our reality. Throughout history, it has been humans' reactions to life that have, through finding solutions and surviving hardships, helped us to evolve and flourish. It's through learning to deal with these difficulties that we have not only become stronger but have been given the opportunity to become more compassionate, understanding, and loving.

Here are a few more NDEs that look at the bad in the world from a different point of view.

(I) *We are on Earth to learn lessons. The bad things that happen aren't caused by God, but by us.*

(II) *We ask, why doesn't God stop the violence?* **Because God didn't start it in the first place.** *When God created us in his image, he unmistakably gave us the power to choose our own destiny. Although not the fate of others.*

The world we live in has been created solely by us. We chose all the hurt, violence, and the pain and suffering. We also chose returns for our sacrifices. Like love and caring, a smile for our loved ones, the perfume of roses, the touch of

157

another, the freedom to be, the wisdom to see ahead, and the fail-safe system so we won't become confused by it all.

(III) *All of my life I was taught that Satan would come for me if I did something bad. But my experience taught me that sin and Satan are our own creations. Freewill, the greatest gift ever given, was there for us to create our own reality. The Earth needs to be brought to an understanding of Oneness and sharing. Now is a time of great need for all to come together as one and help each other.*

It was revealed that **We Are God Experiencing God!**

(IV) *All my life, I've felt confusion and dismay by what I believed was a lack of order. When I saw unnecessary suffering or sadness or things I couldn't make sense of, I'd be riddled with a painful impression of Chaos. I was staggered that the God I so fervently believed in and trusted could do no better than what I was seeing daily.*

During the NDE, I was shown how each individual, through their own freewill, choose paths that…take them to the circumstances of their next existence or life. That nothing at all sits in chaos or lack of order. Every aspect of our lives is controlled by the natural laws that we put ourselves in! We create our worlds. I clearly understood that we can never assume that if someone lives a life of suffering, it's because of their evil deeds.

We can never ever assume that we have the ability to accurately guess why each of us lives the lives we do.

(V) *I instantly was descending like I was in a speeding elevator. The sensation was of going downward and surrounded by total darkness and total silence. When it ended, I found myself in the deepest and darkest void I had or could ever experience. Suddenly, I realized that I was dead. Although I had been created by God. God was a reality, but I was not with him. But it turned out that he was with me. I just did not know that yet. I tried to see but it was too dark. I started hearing noises. What I heard was extremely distressing and eventually became unbearable. As the noise became more intense, I realized it was voices. The innumerable voices of many, souls, saying nothing, only weeping and wailing. It was the most anguished, pathetic sound I had ever heard. It grew with every passing moment, until I imagined their numbers to be in the millions. It felt unbearable. I needed to get out of that place. But how? I had no body nor voice. Finally, from deep within my spirit I screamed as hard as I could. I could hear my bawl echoing on and on, "God, help me!" Within seconds, I felt myself being lifted from that place of pain and sorrow.*

When we boil down the concept of evil, it seems as inevitable as the mistakes and accidents that happen to children learning their way in the world and don't deserve the label "evil." Bit by bit, through experience, we understand which behaviors are to be repeated and which ones are best avoided. Actions that we now think of as wrong or bad are often based on fear, misunderstanding, and frustration.

In chapter 4, on the Life Review, we saw that the Source does not recognize judgment. The Creative Force knows only love and completely and compassionately understands every detail of our position at the time of our act. The Source knows as sure as it knows that we will learn and grow and eventually come home.

15

Choices

In 1969, Peggy Lee sang a song about life titled, *Is That All There Is?* That same question has been asked throughout the ages. Today, we are much more knowledgeable than at any time in the past and have more freedom to explore and create than at any place in history. Young people in schools have become so sophisticated in their learning they easily reach beyond the understanding of some of the great thinkers from yesteryear. Still, to be fair, it is only through the attachment to that historical wisdom that this is possible.

Today, we realize that short of controlling the weather and other people, we are the creators of our lives and the state of the world. Most of us have our heads tucked down in our busy lives, and when we look up to take a breather, we realize things are not what they ought to be and wonder what happened.

Our NDE friends tell us before our birth, we specifically choose the life we are now living. When souls decide to have a physical experience, they first determine a goal or a task they want to accomplish during their lifetime. In some cases, they may come into an Earthly life to help with a specific existing situation and already know what their goals are.

The one thing we can be sure of is their goals are always for the good of the soul's growth and/or the betterment of the world. Once the plan is decided, it becomes the paramount central theme of their lives. All the other choices before entering this existence are based on accomplishing the tasks.

We intentionally aimed ourselves, like a train on a track in the direction that would give us the greatest opportunities to gain what we need to accomplish our soul's task. After all the real purpose of our existence in this world is a spiritual one; to learn our reality, to love one another, and to grow back to our Source.

As if selecting an important outfit from the clothing store we chose our main ensemble, our gender, skin color, ethnicity and our body shape. Then, when we have decided on the basics, we move on to the accessories, the color of our eyes, the shape of our nose, and even the disabilities we will bring into our lives. We even choose the location we will grow up in, our parents, and the general circumstances of our lives. Without fail, each of these choices is an essential tool required to accomplish our task.

Some may wonder how we could have chosen the world we are presently in. Yet, based on information from the other side, that is precisely the reality. While we selected through "freewill," our memories of this process have been erased because we need to come into each life with a clean slate. We need to start fresh and free of old baggage.

While we are still free to choose every aspect of how our lives are lived, it is up to us to make the journey back to the Source quickly or slowly through our attitude, our actions, and even our thoughts.

Once more, we look at comments from those who have returned to share their experiences.

We met **Stella** earlier when she told us of her death when she was hit by a car. She had lost a sandal while crossing the road and went back to get it. Here, she shares with us her understanding of life's choices and how it's connected with life here.

I comprehended that the point of life isn't when time no longer exists but that all the conditions must be satisfied. The most determining is freewill. Our freewill choices and our reactions to events determine the conditions for us to find our destination or miss it. We are so free that we can always try and try again. How long it takes or where it happens doesn't matter because time and space don't exist. The only important thing is to meet the conditions and arrive at the proper destination.

Hafur once more shares with us a wonderful account of her experience. She does not tell us what caused her death except to say that she passed out and died. This lady's experience and her explanation are so beautiful that I recommend everyone take time to read it on the NDERF website.

I saw that I was the one who had designed the life I would have before voluntarily coming into this world. And that my free will within a physical body was found only by consciously nurturing happiness in my thoughts, feelings, and actions. Because I had designed or chosen my destiny before taking on a physical body.

I determined that because I had individually chosen this physical existence, that I had wasted time suffering. When, what I should have been doing, was to use my freedom to choose true love, not pain in all that came into my life.

I understood that there was no judging or punishing God like many religions say there is. It was the expanded consciousness of my mind with an expanded that judged itself and sifted its actions through the filter of perfect, conscious love.

Denise is a woman I found hard not to want to reach out to with compassion and empathy as she shared her story with us. At the time of her death, she was a recently divorced mother of two young boys and working two jobs to make ends meet. When Denise became ill, she was grateful to her neighbor, who offered to help with the kids. Once she knew they were safe and cared for, she lay down and died. Here, she tells us of what she learned about choices.

At that moment, he revealed that his name was John. As we moved, he explained all that was happening. He explained that everyone has choices. Everyone has free will. How this interrelates within our life and death and interconnects with others is all by choice. For example, if the ambulance driver chose to take a different route to an accident scene, if someone decides to move an accident victim who doesn't know what they are doing and causes additional damage, or if the internal organs are too crushed by the accident. Then they will stay here. You are also lying in your son's bedroom and one of your neighbors was given the responsibility to check on you. It is her choice, through her free will, if she finds you. She could decide to have a shower first and be too late. We are constantly caught in a balance through our decisions and by the free will and actions of others.

Patsy doesn't tell us what caused her death**.** She explained that she had been in the hospital for elective surgery because she was continually falling without a reason. She also says that she was raised in a strong Christian tradition and was very active in the church at the time of her experience.

I knew that I had existed since before the moment of creation and I shall always exist. Consciousness is perpetually in the act of becoming. I recognized I had lived many times in a physical reality, and watched those appearances and could observe each of them. I understood what we mean when we say we have free will and that we choose everything. Absolutes do not exist. I witnessed every thought I'd ever chosen to take its natural end and the people it had touched.

I realized that everyone also chooses their own time and the method of their demise.

Through a long conversation, I realized we each chose to come into this life and why we chose our own parents. Those who were anxious and suffered were assisted to see that they chose misery, when they could elect not to suffer because it wasn't necessary.

The idea of choice and freewill does not seem to go together with the notion we are here to accomplish a specific predestined task. If we chose everything right down to the shape of our big toe, it suggests our lives are all packaged up, and there's not much we can do to get away from that fact. But we are also told we do have free choice—lots and lots of it. If we do not like the condition of the world as is, we are free to change it, and more and more people around the world are making that choice.

Although we choose the conditions within our lives, including the location and task(s) we are here to complete, it's up to us when and how we get them done. In accomplishing our chores, we can daydream, sleep, strive, or goof off. It truly does not matter because we will get there eventually, and time is irrelevant at the spiritual level. Although we can take whatever route we want to achieve our mission (including numerous lifetimes). Our effect on others must not delay them from doing what they are here to do. We have no right to hold others back from achieving their goals. However, it does happen repeatedly.

From the soul's perspective, we achieve our personal tasks in our own time and way. Exclusive of the job we do while in the body, what we look like, or our possessions. Love is the one thing we are all here to learn. Love is something we can always give, no matter how rich or poor we are.

It is our choice how we live our lives. It doesn't matter if we commit emotional suicide and give up on life or trudge our way through like a tortoise. We can live dangerously, become the richest person on the planet, or get written up in the history books of all time. These are all just ego desires. At the level of spirit, none of that means anything and is only the zest added to this life for interest's sake. The only thing that matters is to attain our spiritual goals, to learn, to love, and to care for others.

16

Knowledge

Where would we be without human curiosity and our search for knowledge? We would still be living in caves and hunting with clubs and spears. We have come a very long way because of our craving to understand.

Knowledge is a gift that comes through our investigations, explorations, creativity, and inquisitiveness. Humans are not satisfied with simply knowing how something works; we are driven to understand why and for what purpose. The discovery of new things brings excitement and the pleasure of accomplishment. Imagine how it would be to discover that after we die, all knowledge is before us like an extravagant feast of lavish abundance. Imagine that any time we wanted to know something on any subject before we could even think of our questions, the answers came in a flood of brilliant awareness.

Those who returned from an NDE tell us answers were not simply there for them; they were completely immersed in a bottomless ocean of absolute knowing and total understanding on any subject that came to them. It was as if the essence of their being was saturated with profound comprehension of every facet of any question ever asked. NDErs enjoyed a complete understanding of the smallest quantum particle up to the operation of the universe, its origin, and how it evolved to what we are familiar with today.

They were also flooded with knowing how and why we exist and gained an intense appreciation of others to the point that they not only walked in another's shoes but also took a stroll through all that made them who and what they were. NDErs became so close to the person they were thinking of that they knew complete acceptance and unconditional love for them no matter what they had previously thought.

Over and over, those who had an NDE told us of the great depth of awareness they enjoyed. Knowledge, insight, and harmony became a part of what they were. Even more amazing, as people receive the knowledge, realized they already knew the information. Before the questions were asked, the answers were somehow hidden away within them and they had forgotten most of it while in their physical body.

Joann died of a severe asthma attack. While at the spirit level, she was filled with information. She clearly remembers being filled with knowledge. Later, after her return, she continued to remember additional lessons about the universe.

Three sets of beings greeted me. The first group gave me a tour of the whole universe - past, present, and future. The information was injected into me in large sections.

The second set gave me universal knowledge. They implanted everything about creation and how galaxies were created. I had complete understanding about the universe.

The third being was God. I was not allowed further entry and they sent me back.

All my religious questions were also answered. I gained an in-depth understanding about freewill and learned that we have choices about the things that happen. Each of us has both positive and negative events that come out of those choices.

Information was infused into me in large sections. Knowledge became assimilated instantly, and within that minuscule instant everything was completely consumed.

Now, sometimes universal knowledge pops into my head as things occur. For instance, I can remember some physics. When information about black holes hit the papers, I blurted out spontaneously; it's about time they got that figured out.

Michelle saw the car racing toward her and put her hand out as if to stop it. The next second, she was in another dimension. Her experience was almost textbook classic as she met other beings, had a life review, and gained deep knowledge that filled her to the brim.

Questions poured from me about life, and I received instant answers. No words were necessary, yet understanding of life, God, and all that is became crystal clear. It felt like I was being reintroduced or awakened after a long, hard sleep. I thought the questions and the understanding flooded me.

We will hear more from Michele in the chapter on Returning.

Brian had an NDE because of a car accident. An elderly couple was coming onto a highway from a side road and ran through the stop sign.

Unexpectedly, I realized I had complete knowledge. There were no more questions; total knowledge instantly arrived. Every aspect of creation was part of one ginormous concept. I explored these enormous concepts from the inside and I became everything the instant I thought of it.

Geralyn was thirteen years old when she died from Burkett's lymphoma, a form of cancer. In the middle of an operation on her intestines, she died and later was able to tell the doctors exactly what they were doing during the procedure. Although her details were correct, the doctors chose not to believe her. It was shortly after watching the operation from above that she suddenly found herself filled with an understanding of things she had never even thought of asking.

As I began to rise, all at once it seemed as though I knew everything there was to know. It felt like every mystery of the world was being revealed. I totally understood science, math, and life's questions!

It felt as though I knew everything that could be known. It all became so clear and understandable.

Bridget was in a serious car accident in which her vehicle rolled and landed on top of her, and she died. Bridget tells us a delightful account of how she had always known the Creator because, as a child, she used to play games with God by asking questions about the universe and then flying through the cosmos to find the answer. For that reason, when she died she wasn't surprised to find herself filled with vast amounts of knowledge.

Then, I became extremely excited and started asking questions like a curious child. I wanted to know about aliens, parallel universes, of life on other planets, and UFOs and, and, and... Then, I sensed a great, yet quiet, chuckle of amusement, like a parent's pat on the head. I saw from the beginning of the beginning of everything and nothing. I saw the entire universe from the big bang to big stop, to the big bang and the big stop; I had full memory of the universe. Wisdom of cosmology, biology, spiritualism, consciousness, being, non-being, physics, and mathematics and more. Essentially, I knew everything there was to know and unknow. The Source is everything that can ever, has ever been, and can never be simultaneously. I'm human and can only understand in human terms. Even the greatest of humanity is still human, and everything was anthropomorphic.

Wayne shared his experience with us earlier. He was pushing a car when another car slammed into him. The next thing, he woke up on a gurney and knew he was going to die and welcomed the relief from the pain. Raised as a Southern Baptist, Wayne tells us, at death, he expected to find a man in a white robe sitting on a golden throne there to greet him. Instead, he floated in darkness briefly and then saw what he calls a silver river of sparkling colors.

A strong desire pushed me to join the river of life. It felt like home. This was where I came from and belonged. When I touched the river I gained insights into realms beyond realms, universes beyond universes, and dimensions beyond dimensions. I knew infinity.

There was an infinite number of domains of existence, and all were a part of the Source. The stream offered distinct levels that weren't divided by any barrier. Each layer seemed to have a different density. The stream of consciousness and knowledge may be the mind of god.

Every aspect of these reports brings new questions that pester us, like a persistent child tugging at their parents for attention. How is it possible for people to suddenly have all the wisdom flow through them after death? Where did the information originate? Why is it that we gain knowledge while we are dead and not while we are in the body? Why are these people not able to remember this knowledge when they return?

Perhaps we don't remember this great knowledge while we are here for several reasons. If we knew every answer to every question while physical, then, the purpose of being human would be lost. If we were here to learn and grow in love back to the Source, then, total understanding would negate that goal.

Given the reports from NDErs, we are here to serve the Creator's purposes, and it is essential that we come here to find the answers to our questions on our own. If we already knew everything, there would be no learning and growth in understanding.

As a species, we are worse than the curious cat. We will go anywhere and do anything to get answers to our questions. As though overwhelmed by an itch or craving, we lust after answers to sate our driving hunger. We strive to complete a task with vigor and determination. Once we have the answers to our satisfaction, we bless them with gratitude for all we've gained and tuck them away where they are handy for future use. Then, we move on to the next undertaking. Through learning, we see that one thing relates to another that links to another. The drive for awareness and understanding never ends.

17

Purpose

Questions about how we differ from the other creatures of the world have pushed us to find distinctions. For centuries, we took smug comfort in our superiority because we thought we were the only living species on Earth with a soul.

As we become closer to nature, we discover so much more about the other friends that share the planet with us. This deeper understanding spans both scientific and spiritual perspectives. Science has learned that several animal species have a form of communication that brings a level of reasoning and planning previously not realized. Spiritually, the world is finding deep connections between all expressions of life.

It is interesting, then, to realize there is one area of distinction between other life forms and us. Humans operate much better when there is a purpose to our lives. Our desire for meaning offers us the opportunity to dream and strive toward a goal. With aspirations, we can make sense of our existence and satisfy an inner yearning to know. Without purpose, we question our existence: "Why was I born? What am I supposed to do here in this life? Do I have a purpose?" And, closely related to these is the question at the base of them all; "Do I matter?"

Those with no goals are generally less enthusiastic about life. Some may become restless and try dangerous activities to fill the void. In contrast, others may become lethargic blobs of nothingness with no direction. These sad souls go to work, do what they must do, and come home to the internet or television. And wish the world would just leave them alone.

While we are here in a physical existence, our feelings of separateness from our Source are enhanced and produce a sense of isolation for some. At the spiritual level, an awareness of purpose often fills that gap. It brings a perception of closeness to the world and spirit.

In reading the NDE contributions, we learn that everyone on Earth is here for a reason. This purpose is rarely the same for everyone. Some people are here to teach or create, others may dedicate themselves to the service of others, and some are on a spiritual quest. It may also be true some are here to know the loneliness of mental illness, addiction, or living on the street. Although there are numerous directions we can go, there is one purpose we all share: to love and care for one another. Love is one thing that is free for us to give.

Each time we see the mind-boggling poverty of the world or know about people dying because of lack, we are offered an opportunity to reach out in caring, thus helping one another and ourselves to get a step closer to the peace, joy, and love that is ours. As Oprah has frequently said, every disagreement, disappointment, or cruelty, small or large, is another opening to speed up our growth back to our Source. She suggests we ask ourselves, *what is the learning in this situation for me?*

Bill went to the doctor because he had trouble doing things without feeling exhausted. He quickly learned his heart was in bad shape, and he needed an immediate bypass. During the operation, he died twice and found himself in a picturesque garden. While there, three entities joined him and offered him a choice to stay or return to his body. However, he was told that he had a job to do if he chose to go back.

I knew I could choose to stay if I wanted, or I could return. If I returned, there were some tasks I needed to do. I elected to come back and finish my chores.

My children had a big part of my coming back. As happy as I was there, uncontrollable sadness overcame me. I remembered I hadn't said goodbye to my children.

Bill died a second time and arrived at the doorway to the same garden he had been in before. However, this time, he was not allowed in. His grandmother greeted him and escorted him back to his body. When he arrived, he knew his new purpose in life.

I knew that my mission was to work with children. I needed to open a dungeon and dragons' den. On June 22, 2002 (on the summer solstice), Cody's Castle was opened.

This next NDEr has an interesting identification; he calls himself **a soldier.** His NDE happened in the middle of a war. He tells us he had become a mean and tough person who trained Green Berets and knew how to kill with every part of his body. He also tells us that he cared nothing for the enemy as human beings. The higher the kill count, the better. Eventually, he was killed by a mortar shell. He immediately found himself in a horrible hell experience that would have been worse than any horror movie created. He was eventually saved by a close friend who had died a year before this soldier's death.

Hey, there, my friend said, I know that was brutal, but you needed it. You were getting just a bit too callous, and that isn't like you. At least, that wasn't the guy I knew when we played football and hung out in high school.

The incredible beauty of where we stood put me in a state of awe. It was peaceful a meadow with a sparkling stream running through it. The colors were far more vivid than on Earth.

That's when I noticed that my friend was glowing. I looked at myself and I had a bit of a glow, too. My friend told me I wasn't doing the right thing. Your mission is to help and to protect others. You need to return to your life. You will come back here, but right now, you must go back and discover your complete mission.

Our soldier friend understandably became much more compassionate toward the women and children of the country he was battling. When he went back home, he studied to become a teacher and volunteered to build shelters for abused women and their children.

Sammy had a heart attack while in the middle of a cardiac stress test. Fortunately, he was surrounded by medical personnel and able to get immediate help, but not before he had an NDE. After his tunnel experience, he was met by his deceased first wife and found himself in a beautiful garden. At that point, he was joined by another entity who talked to him about his life's purpose.

There was someone I spoke with for hours. We discussed why we are here and my plans for this life. During our talk, it felt like I knew it all. The meaning of life and what it's all about. I learned there's a master plan where every soul has a part. Each aspect of the plan is of equal importance. The human belief that position and status makes us more valuable than others is just egotistical nonsense. I remember thinking that way, too.

Lisa, a five-year-old Russian girl, was spending a day with her family at the beach. Her mother's arms cuddled her as they sat at the shore and allowed the waves to wash over them. Suddenly, Lisa tells us, a huge wave crashed on them, and she was swept out of her mother's arms and out to sea where she drowned. Lisa had an extensive experience and years later, she clearly remembers what she learned during her NDE.

I was told that it wasn't my time. I had simply been granted a visit back home. But I had to return and fulfill my purpose and do what I had promised to do on Earth. The being of light reminded me that I was to learn more about love and compassion and how best to express them here on Earth. My work was also to help other people however I could. I had chosen this myself. The voice told me that I would be back in the world of light in no time. Don't forget that there is no time, only eternity.

S was doing veterinarian work when a horse became frightened, reared up, hit her on the head, and caused severe injuries. During her death experience, she was able to learn her purpose and the results of fear.

I remember an almost tangible absence of all fear. I understood that fear is behind so many of our poor choices when, in reality, there is nothing to fear. I felt compassion for myself that I never imagined possible. It was a love that I had never known. Empathy, compassion for my life, and determination to live as I could, should, and must. I realized that I had a purpose and they showed it to me so I could understand how needed I was. I had no pain. I'm unsure if my guides or I had a body. It didn't matter.

A vast amount of information flooded me, and I had total understanding of everything. I connected with the importance of my life's purpose. Although I saw the future, I don't remember it. I knew how difficult my recovery was going to be after the accident. Although I would get through it, the main point was to do what I was here to do. But I could only serve my purpose if I lost my fear of rejection, of not being liked for the stands I took, feeling like I didn't have control of things, etc. Only then could I act out of pure love with no complications or compromises. Once my understanding was complete, I was back in my body in excruciating pain.

Each of us has a purpose that is as critical as everyone else's. There are no "small or insignificant" lives—we are all connected. Like having a small role in a play—it might not be as noticeable as the lead, but the story needs every player to do their specific and equally critical role.

S2, this person had surgery on their stomach, and while recovering, developed peritonitis. Instinctively, they knew that the end was near. Although this report is brief, what we learn from their NDE is enlightening.

The voice told me that I had a very special purpose and must always be true to myself. Before my illness I was a rock musician even though I couldn't read or write music. Later, after my recovery, I sat down one night at my piano and fell asleep. When I woke up ten hours later, there was a completed symphony I had written. Since then, I've become an accomplished classical composer and conductor. I play the role of "spirit guide" to many people.

It is possible that this person didn't include a name for privacy because it is well known.

Ron was a young teen out drinking with three of his buddies. On the way home, they got into an accident, and he died. While Ron was on the other side, he learned several interesting lessons. Here is what he shares with us about the purpose of life.

The main purpose of life is our spiritual growth. Put simply, that's the process of learning about the wisdom and power of universal, unconditional love. The various religions get in the way with their judgments and lessons of separation. In the end, all that actually matters are people and our relationship with them.

Based on these reports, we come here with a specific purpose tucked under our arms that we chose before coming into the world. However, we have ultimate freedom and can put our feet up and be as lazy as we want. We are the ones to decide how we live this life. If we don't complete our task now, it simply stays there like the dishes stacked in the sink until we are ready to do it, no matter how many lifetimes that takes.

18

Responsibility and Freedom

Today, more than at any time in history, we have the freedom to live our lives as we choose. Generally, we are better educated and have a clearer understanding of what's happening in the world and our roles in it than at any time in the past.

The internet has opened doors not only to wealthy countries but to poorer nations as well. And while we must be mindful of the quality of knowledge to color our views, there are numerous excellent, high-quality sites where we can acquire remarkable information.

To speak about responsibility and freedom, I must take a small sidestep away from NDEs. For thirty years, I was a family counselor. A large part of my job was helping parents deal with children's behavior issues.

Responsibility is as vital for children to learn as being able to dress themselves or learn a basic education. And, like those things, taking the consequences for one's actions must be taught. It isn't an instinct that kids are born with. It means falling and skinning their knees, making mistakes, and, at times, fumbling their way in the dark. It also requires supportive, loving adults nearby to guide them through the tough spots before they turn into a knotted mess.

One day, when my children were very little, my mother said two things about child raising that I never forgot. She said she raised us kids to be responsible adults, not immature children. And adults have many more years of experience to know what is best, so no child would tell her what to do.

It is gratifying for kids when they experience the consequences of their actions. It is not a punishment but an opportunity to learn and be better adults. It's through undergoing what happens from their activities that children can make better choices in the future.

We are talking about simple common sense. If the child breaks it, they either fix it or replace it. If they can't replace it, they can do chores around the house to work it off. If they make a mess, they clean it up. And allow them to do as many things for themselves as possible so that they have those skills in the future. Common sense parenting also helps the young person to become more confident and secure within themselves.

Generally, when people talk about responsibility, they think of the heavy weight of things they must do, whether they want to or not. The word comes with big sighs and obligations.

There's another side to the issue that often is not realized. Responsibility is the flip side of freedom. You can't have one without the other. We all love freedom. It is the milk to go with the honey. Things don't work well when this is the only side of this duo that we are willing to consider.

Freedom to do our own thing comes with responsibility for the outcome. And in turn, taking full accountability brings freedom because we know what can and can't be done. We become more confident in our abilities and trust ourselves more. Leading to even more freedom.

Now, we return to NDEs and the lessons within those experiences. Repeatedly, I hear people say that everything is meant to be and there are no mistakes. Where is the freedom and responsibility?

Indeed, many elements are decided before we come to this life, as we spoke about in the chapter on Purpose. But we must mix it with one hundred percent freewill. That means we can change any part at any point in our lives.

The purpose of our physical existence has many goals: to discover our reality, to Love one another, and to grow back to our Source, as well as a possible specific task we have taken on.

Although we made a deal to achieve a task, we can take as long as we want. We can take one lifetime or twenty. That's up to us. Time has no meaning for the Source.

Earlier in this book, I pointed out that some NDErs are asked, "What have you done with your life?" In each case, that question causes the individual to feel bad that they have done nothing in their life and have not done anything toward their goal. I wonder about all the people who are not doing anything toward their goal but have not had an NDE push in that direction? How many people have turned off life and are just putting in the time until the end?

Another aspect of life that interferes with our accomplishing our goal is other people. It's at this point that we can get dizzy. We have no control over other people's choices. If our goal is attached to another person who doesn't or couldn't follow through on their goal. Then, we would have to wait until our next incarnation when we have another chance.

Then again, the chosen task may be too large to complete in one lifetime. We may need two or three lifetimes to have it completed.

Nothing is permanent, including those goals we so carefully set for ourselves. Dannion Brinkley was a mercenary in the US military. In his book *Saved by the Light*, he tells us that during his life review, he was asked why he'd killed a certain man? He learned that person had a job to do, and now he would have to start over again before it could be done.

Another woman in an abusive relationship was asked what she had learned while she was dead. She responded that she'd always had freewill to choose differently.

The moment we refuse our responsibility, we also deny our freedom. Thinking that everything is meant to be turns us into victims. Then, we can't take authorship of our roles or learn from them. Nor can we enact changes to help the situation. This includes the delightfully kind and giving acts as well as the bad.

It could also be extrapolated to why bother at all? If it's meant to be, then why have spiritual goals? Why step in when we see injustices? We could just shrug our shoulders and walk away because it was written in the wind.

There is a direct correlation between freedom and happiness. When we understand our role in creating situations we find ourselves in, then we are more able to perceive an alternate. When responsibility is enmeshed with our freedom, everything changes. Even people who live under a dictatorship have freedom. It may be more limited than we would like, but freewill is still present.

Victor Frankl, in his book Man's Search for Meaning, talks about being in a concentration camp during WWII. While there, he realized that we each have a specific element of ourselves deep within. That unique aspect is ours alone, and no matter what may be done to us, it's up to us to give it or not. When we give away our freedom and responsibility, we give away our power as well.

Frankl talked about the freedoms enjoyed under these extremely limiting conditions. They called others out from the barracks to watch the beautiful sunset, or they marveled and found hope for the world through a crocus coming up through the snow. That's a pretty cool mentality in a concentration camp.

Today, more and more of us realize we decide how much authority we want to give this illusion called life. We have enough information to make up our minds about our reality. We can no longer blame another for taking over our lives, kidnapping our senses, and controlling our behavior. We can finally enjoy freedom and responsibility in joy.

Throughout human existence, we have demonstrated an incredible ability to create, starting with the primitive tools held by furry creatures destined to be our ancestors. Today, our creativity shows itself in stunning architecture, transportation, and countless inventions, along with art, music, dance, writing, and remarkable philosophical and scientific concepts.

Confusion on this point is understandable. Some NDErs have returned from death, saying there are no accidents, or it's meant to be. Confusion reigns because this is true. They are speaking at the spirit level. There, we are the Creator having an experience of being physical. Time is irrelevant, and this existence is an illusion.

Here are a few comments on freewill.

Malla suffered from a chronic illness and was fed up with constantly fighting pain. While at the spirit level, she learned we create what we know.

We were given a wonderous gift. We launched ourselves into physical form. Our thoughts are extremely powerful. They shape our bodies and our lives to fit our core beliefs. We are here to experience joy and Love. Instead of the hardship our lives have become. This life we are living is a direct outcome of what we think about. It is essential to let go of fear because it's the foundation of all suffering.

After his car accident, **Ron** realized languages separated and divided us and brought fundamental loneliness. [This can also be true even when we speak the same vocabulary.]

In this life we are emotionally and intellectually separated from our spiritual connection to Source. This brings about loneliness and fear. Fear causes us to become fearful and judgmental because our senses, intelligence, and what we learn from others is where we place intention. We believe in this existence so deeply that it has become our sole reality. There is a straight line between what happens for us and the choices we make both individually and as a society. Thus, it's the cycle of responsibility and freedom.

After **Stella** returned from death, she shared how our choices connected with the life we experience here.

The most crucial aspect of our lives is our freewill choices and reactions. They determine our ability to complete what we are here to accomplish. And because time is irrelevant to the spirit level, it doesn't matter how long we take. We can take multiple lives to accomplish our goals. The only condition is to arrive at the proper destination.

Although **Cara** doesn't tell us what caused her death, she is very clear when talking about choices.

I was given an option to return or stay. I knew if I didn't return, I would return to another life to complete my goal. I also realized that everything was well planned, and it was up to me how I used it. Even when another's preplanned path crossed mine, I could choose to disregard the opportunity or be open to the opportunities offered.

Hafur saw that she designed the life she would live.

There were no judgments that dictated what I was to do. Only my mind, with an expanded consciousness, was the controlling factor. Decisions were made through the filter of perfect, conscious Love.

I had directly chosen to become a physical body and have these life experiences. I realized that I had wasted time suffering when I should have been using my freedom to choose to love not pain in everything that came into my life.

I saw that it was I who designed the life I would eventually lead before willingly entering this existence. Further, that my freedom within this physical life would be found only by consciously cultivating happiness in all aspects of my life. I was the one who designed amd chosen my destiny before taking on this physical body.

Mellen-Thomas Benedict had an astonishing death experience, and I encourage everyone to read it online by searching his name. Before his death, he was bitter and angry and thought people were a cancer in the world. His extensive experience took him to the universe's beginning, where he learned how it all began. Benedict also returned with a rare gift. He remembered a great deal of what he had learned while on the other side. There are several inventions based on his understanding of how everything went together.

While at the spirit level, I saw people's souls and was shocked to see there were no evil souls anywhere. I asked if mankind could be saved. His guide responded, "Remember this and never forget, you save, redeem, and heal yourself. You always have. You always will. There is no such place as outward, only inward. Thoughts are very powerful, and as you think, so you are."

The idea of freewill may not go together with the notion we are here to accomplish predestined tasks and that our lives are well-planned. If we choose everything, that concept suggests our lives are packaged, and there's not much we can do to escape that fact. But we do have free choice—lots and lots of it. If we don't like the condition of the world, we're at liberty to change it. More and more people around the world are making that choice.

If we are one with the Loving Light, it makes sense that at death, we would gain the same deep and intimate comprehension of all knowledge. That comprehension would be an understanding of our own being, answers to the deepest mysteries of physics, and entire awareness of all life. If we are indivisible from the Source, as Oneness states, it follows that there would be nothing that was beyond our comprehension or our abilities.

Although we select the conditions within our lives, we can take whatever route we want to accomplish our mission, including numerous lifetimes. It's important to consider others in our decisions so we don't delay them from doing what they are here to do. To that end, we must fulfill our responsibilities and follow through with our promises.

Love is the one thing we are all here to learn. It is something we can give, no matter how rich or poor we are.

19

Reincarnation

The debate over whether we live a single life or more than one has been ongoing for centuries. Most of us can't remember another life, so we either don't know what to believe or completely reject the idea.

We may ask, "Why live more than once? This life is hard enough without doing it again?" Whether a person believes in reincarnation or not if given a choice, most of us would vote not to return to another life in the physical. Yet we are told by our NDE friends that returning souls are overjoyed to come back.

At one time, the Eastern religions believed that we returned, while Judaic faiths did not. However, over the last fifty years, there has been a shift. Today, large numbers of Western thinking are accepting reincarnation as a reality.

Psychiatrist Ian Stevenson from the University of Virginia[23] is famous for his research on reincarnation and is highly respected for his dedication to the scientific method of research and documentation. He spent forty years researching reincarnation and studied 2,500 cases to conclude, at least for him, that it was a reality.

Dr. Kenneth Ring,[24] Dr. Erlander Haraldsson, Dr. Jim B Tucker,[25] and Dr. Brian Weiss[26] are some of the other people who have also researched the subject.

We are intrigued to learn more about our past lives. Who were we, where did we live, what did we do? Yet, from the spiritual position, the major question is, why? What possible reason would the spirit have to come back and live another life here on Earth or anywhere else in the universe?

The Eastern religions say we return to clear up our karma. Those NDErs who have returned with an understanding of reincarnation agree they have returned to complete unfinished business. However, that is about as far as the similarities go. Eastern thinking attaches negative connotations to unfinished karma.

Once more, we will look at some of the reports on reincarnation from those who learned about this aspect of the spiritual.

Thomas died when the pickup truck he was driving landed on his chest and crushed him.[27] Before this, as a devout atheist, he did not believe in life after death. At the time of his death, he woke up in total darkness with all his normal senses intact. The moment Thomas began to wonder where he was, a tunnel appeared, inviting him to enter. Soon, he was traveling at the speed of light down the tunnel into a place of overwhelming love. Here is what he tells us about incarnating into another life.

Reincarnation is an opportunity to reach an ultimate goal. That objective being the realization that you are a soul and One of God, as well as the universe. Few of us have a positive image of their soul. We blind ourselves to ninety-five percent of our truth as soul. It is necessary to reincarnate to discover all that we are.

Amy shared her life review with us above. She was the young woman who suffered from a severe case of fibromyalgia and died from an accidental overdose of painkillers. Amy was raised to believe that God allowed pain to happen as a test of how strong we were. Here, she tells us of her new understanding of reincarnation.

During my NDE, I realized that most of us have lived much, much longer than we could even thought possible. Our lives may feel very long yet are infinitesimal when placed in the whole picture. For that matter, the vastness of eternity cannot even be related. Every individual, through their own freewill, chooses the paths that will take them to the conditions of their next existence. Every aspect of our lives is ruled by the laws of nature that we place upon ourselves! We each create our own worlds.

I knew that one can never assume that someone's suffering is because of their evil deeds. Many souls elect a life of misery in search of what it awakens in them or to help another, etc. Nor can we assume that we have the ability to accurately guess why each being lives the life they live.

I can't describe the liberation...the refreshing, peaceful salve this wisdom brought me. Finally, I gained a truth that I had yearned for all my life. I knew that all is good! There is *a sense of order and beauty all around. No one is in free-fall as it seemed to me before! That God does not just toy with us as He pleases through scattered tests of us. And then include rewards and punishments that depend simply upon His current mood or mindset.*

John was a young man who suffered from severe asthma. He got a cold, and one lung collapsed while he was sleeping. At first, John thought he was dreaming that he had died in a fall. It didn't take long for him to realize this was not a dream and he was dead. After a short time of floating in darkness John saw a light approaching, and it turned into Jesus. But he was confused because Jesus was calling him Jim, not John. In his bewilderment, he asked Jesus about this. Let's peek in on their conversation.

Something compelled me to ask if reincarnation was true. If yes, then, I wanted to know if I reincarnated, and who was I. Jesus explained yes to both questions. He said that I had indeed reincarnated. He stressed that was not important. I then asked if I was Jim Morrison, the singer of the Doors, for don't know why I asked that—something I now think as weird because I knew next to nothing about him before the NDE. Yet again he said it was not important because reincarnation isn't as we understand it.

That's when our communication became nonverbal. Knowledge poured into me at a rapid pace. I realized that even though we reincarnate, it is always the same soul in a different shell. The focus should not be on who I used to be because I'm still the same soul.

(There are other NDEs where the person is called by a different name than their present name in this life. I don't know what that means, other than another identity, perhaps through reincarnation or it may be that the soul has a name apart from the diverse shells it wears.)

Sandra fell off a cliff when a rock she was standing on crumbled under her, and she tumbled about sixty-five feet. At the beginning of her fall, she thought that she was going to die. Then, Sandra was above her body as she watched it flip over and over until it landed face down in water. Although Sandra doesn't tell us her age, she does say she was a child at the time.

This NDE taught me about reincarnation. Although I'd never heard of reincarnation, since I returned, I cannot accept any other belief system. Now I know reincarnation is real and that we have lessons we need to learn during each lifetime. If we don't absorb the lessons, we need to go through life after life until we get it. I think the curtain between life and death is very thin.

Cara had an accident and fractured her skull and severed arteries in her brain, that caused bleeding. She was given a craniotomy to correct the condition and then floated between life and death for two days. Here, Cara tells us what she learned about reincarnation.

Focus was placed upon each life experience, while all the events contribute to an accumulated final result. I was unhappy about returning to Earth. However, after discussions with beings of energy, including God, we decided that my return would serve the greater good. Although I had a choice, somehow the decision was made together with other beings. I

197

knew that if I didn't return at this time, in this body, I would have to reincarnate to the Earth school in another body to finish what I came here to do. Before the experience, I had little thought of reincarnation. Now, I'm sure that I have had many incarnations.

There is no personal information about this next individual or about what caused their death. This case comes from a study done by Dr. Kenneth Ring in 1993 and was published in the *Journal of Near-Death Studies.*

My whole life was before me. Everything I have ever done or didn't do. Not just within this one lifetime, but all the lifetimes. Now, I know for a fact that reincarnation is true. It is absolute. I understood that throughout them all, I had overcome and gained some knowledge. In other lives there were still things to be learned.

This next woman is from a study done by Dr. Melvin Morse.[28] He reports that the woman committed suicide by shooting herself in the head. But instead of the oblivion she sought, she found herself in a brilliant, loving light she identified as Jesus. The light being went through a life review with her and then talked about her choices.

She had access to unlimited knowledge. She was told that she could remain in the light, but she needed to understand that she would reincarnate and re-experience and all that brought her to the point of suicide and find a way to work it out. Or she could return and live out the rest of her life and conquer her problems here and now. Obviously, she chose not to stay in the light so that she could resume her life and not have to face the same difficulties in a future life.

Rev. Irving S. Cooper's book, *Reincarnation: A Hope of the World*, gives an excellent overview of the study of reincarnation.[29] Here is a summary on the subject.

The chief purpose of reincarnation is education. To this end, we are born again and again on Earth, not because of any external pressure but because we, as souls, desire to grow.

It's a universal process and prevails not only in the human kingdom but also throughout the whole of nature. Whenever we find a living body, the consciousness of that form is also evolving, using the physical universe temporarily for that purpose. The corporeal form is so that it may gain physical experience. In each incarnation, we have a different physical body and name. There may be a variety of souls acting as parents, but these changes don't even slightly imperil our individuality. However, reincarnation is not an endless process. When we've learned the lessons taught in the World-School, we will return no more to physical incarnation unless we willingly come back to act as Teachers of humanity or as Helpers in a glorious plan of evolution.

It seems irrelevant whether reincarnation is real or not. During our time in the physical dimension, we have numerous experiences to help us learn and grow. If there were no deaths, then life would simply be a continuum of being without the learning and growth we enjoy in between lives. For now, we are here, and it is here that we should place our attention.

One might argue that by knowing our past life, we can recognize what we are here to learn. In some cases, this may be true if we are stuck in our development. Otherwise, our souls already know what we came here to learn. At that level, we have brought information about our past life into our present existence.

Additionally, we are repeatedly told, here and in other places, that our mission is to love and care for one another. Yet our obsession with the material simply distracts us from that goal. Then we miss our mark and must do it all over again.

20

Returning

Thoughts of those we love can melt us into affectionate teddy bears stuffed with tender emotions. When we think of losing them in death, we are filled with pain, loneliness, and fear. It may seem strange to realize this is not what is reported by those who have died and returned. The simple truth is the majority did not want to come back.

NDErs tell us they became like children who had been let loose in a toy store only to learn it was time to go home. Many pleaded, argued, and became angry and even frightened when they realized they were required to return. The overwhelming unconditional love, peace, and joy that became a part of their being in the afterlife compelled them to reach out in longing to stay.

Rejection and a sense of desertion came to some of those who did not want to come back. To be fair, many do return specifically for the sake of their loved ones. Yet a large portion of NDErs returned to their bodies wrapped in disappointment, depression, and even anger at being sent back. The point is not that their love for us has stopped. Quite the opposite. They have been injected with so much love that it overflows from them like a fountain. Their love quotient has multiplied like prairie dogs in spring, and they realize that love is the main element of life. Their love for us had not stopped but, in the other dimension, they saw things from a completely different perspective.

An overwhelming number were told to return to the physical and finish the tasks they had come to complete. There was no shirking these responsibilities agreed upon before their birth.

Not all returned because of unfinished tasks. There were other reasons for coming back to this life. A large percentage willingly returned because of their children and other loved ones. Sometimes, people were shown that one or more of their children would run into future difficulties and would need their help. At other times, the person having the NDE was asked to bring back the knowledge they had gained on the other side while others return to tell the world of their experience.

Here are a few people telling of their return.

(NB: This next case is very difficult for me, and I assume for most of us. This soul did indeed choose a difficult life. I debated about including it because of the pain it might bring to the reader. But, decided that it was also a part of the NDE experience.)

C tells us she had already experienced numerous traumas of severe child abuse by the time she was five. After being admitted to the hospital emergency from a beating, she died. Her family were strong Christians, and she understood the concept of angels, so she wasn't surprised when she was greeted by an angel. Although she wrote her account as an adult, she remembered the event as though it had just happened.

The angel explained that the physical world belongs to us material beings. All life, humans, animals, plants are physical and are subject to the laws of this physical realm. However, the physical realm is not all that exists. She wanted me to understand that she and the others there were ethereal beings. Therefore, they couldn't influence the physical realm. The angel clarified that they couldn't stop the people from hurting me. But, while she explained it, I knew that the pain I endured hurt her, too. She was totally empathetic, and I realized they would always be with me. She explained that, while they couldn't stop what was happening, they would always be there and witness everything. I appreciated that I would always have contact with someone who fully understood what I had been through. She insisted I understand that because they are not of the physical realm, we needed to be sensitive to relate with them. They can then converse and affect people (or animals) of this realm. We can then impact the world around us.

G shot herself in an attempt to commit suicide. Although she does not share her reasons for wanting to die, she says she arrived in a beautiful garden with several lovely people. Nearby, she could see a well or hole, which she ignored. She was very happy where she was until it became clear she was being sent back through that hole.

After I spent time with my guides, I felt a strong force push me toward a hole or well. I grasped the rim of the well with all my strength to fight something that was pulling me downward. I was running out of strength to hold myself back and held out my hands so the guides could catch me and help pull me back up. But they just waved goodbye to me. I yelled to them not to let me go. I shouted that if they were good, why didn't they help me to stay. I wanted to be with them. But a force continued to pull me down. Beyond my control, I kept going down until I opened my eyes and realized I was back in this world again. I was so cold. I didn't like this existence and began crying that I wanted to go back to where I had been.

Over time, I learned that we are visiting this life, We are here to learn, and the best is yet to come after this life.

It took G several years before she accepted this is where she is to be. She tells us she has finally found peace within herself about this reality.

Nancy was at the dentist's office when she died from an overdose of nitrous oxide coupled with her air supply somehow being cut off by the face mask. She was an acquaintance of the dentist and knew he had a cocaine problem. While out of her body, Nancy floated over the Earth before arriving in a beautiful place filled with golden light. There, she met Scott, a friend who had committed suicide. Shortly after she learned she had to return and finish her life on Earth.

My friend, Scott, explained that I'd gone too far. I needed to turn around and go back right away. There were many more things I had to do before I could go back there. With a fatherly chuckle as if I was a rambunctious child going there before my time. I still had a long and interesting life ahead of me. There were things that needed attention of before returning.

As I turned around toward the direction of Earth, I could hear the dentist begging me to come back. My heart felt sorry for him and I immediately shot back into my body. When my spirit reentered my body, I didn't fit anymore. I had become a little ball in chest. I had to work hard to force myself to take my first breath. It was the hardest thing I've ever done! A moment later I gasped my first breath, my spirit instantaneously filled my body from top to bottom.

Duane was a single parent who belonged to a group that went rafting every weekend with their children. Although he had just finished working a double shift and had been awake for twenty-four hours. He didn't want to disappoint his children, and decided to push himself just a little bit more. Duane went rafting with the group without a lifejacket, even though he knew better. Once they started, he allowed the girls to handle the raft and snuggled down for a nap. Two hours later, he was shocked to find himself dumped into the rapids, and after a struggle, he drowned. Shortly after dying, he was amazed to have a life review and then was asked a question.

Awe filled me as I witnessed all that was happening. A voice as clear as one standing beside me asked if I wanted to say there of return to my life.

At this point, Duane chose to stay in the sublime feeling of love and calm peace and immediately saw his oldest daughter as she searched for him.

Immediately, it was as if someone had grabbed hold of me and thrown me inside my oldest daughter. I could see from her eyes and hear what she heard. I understood everything from her point of view. It felt like I was a bystander in her world. My twelve-year-old daughter, was faced with a dreadful situation, was so calm and logical as anyone could possibly be under those conditions.

My youngest daughter has also fallen from the raft and caught in the same undertow. But she was wearing a life jacket and was safe. My oldest daughter's thoughts were clear. She reasoned that her sister and the others were ok. Now she needed to save me. Then, instantly I was back in my own consciousness floating above the water. Once more the voice asked me what I wanted to do. Ultimately, I realized that I needed to choose between staying there or returning to raise my daughters and complete life in this body.

No one pressured me to choose either way. Neither was I led to believe there was value to my decision. The choice was wholly up to me. I realized that my daughters needed me and how much I loved them. I decided to come back and do everything within my power to raise them the best I could.

Then, the voice said that I had to give the job all I had to give. Then I understood that I had to choose to be in my body because no one was going to put me there. This communication was shoved at me with the urgency a father might have for a child in immediate danger. Once having made the conscious choice to be in my body I once more felt the water erupting around me.

Anthony had an accident while riding his motorcycle and, because he was not wearing a helmet, suffered severe brain damage. He was fortunate that a paramedic immediately gave him CPR, and minutes later, he was hospitalized. Fortune further shone on him as there was a convention of neurosurgeons in the city that just happened to be at the hospital when Anthony arrived. With all that help, he still managed to be clinically dead for thirty-three minutes and was greeted by his family and Jesus. Here, he talks about meeting Jesus and his return to the physical world.

When I looked to locate where the light was coming from, I saw Jesus floating toward me on a beam of light. He looked intensely at me and asked what I was going to do. I was surprised that I had a choice and asked him about it.

Jesus told me that I had been badly hurt in the accident and no one would blame me if I stayed there.

My thoughts turned to all the people that I care so much about. Jesus put his hand on my shoulder and turned me around. Telepathically he told me to look down. I saw everybody I loved and cared about. They were deeply saddened and lost. I realized this is what my death would do to the people I loved.

Then, magically he opened them up to show me their hearts. I saw my wife, mother, stepchildren, and siblings. Their hearts looked like they had been torn, and pieces dripped down. Jesus clarified that their hearts were breaking. He explained that this was what the future would be without me in their lives."

With this information, the choice was no longer hard. I had to go back. That's when I heard the prayers of everyone who cared about me. I heard their thoughts and prayers as if they were right there beside me.

I told Jesus that I wanted to go back. I had the impression that Jesus approved of my decision because he told me that it was not my time to be there. That he had bigger, better things planned for me.

After I returned, I closed my construction company and began working in the social service field. I now work with disadvantaged children and families, to help them overcome the obstacles that stand in their way. I want to make their lives more complete and happier. I'm good at what I do and that's what God wanted me to do.

Nancy was a twelve-year-old girl at a slumber party when she left her body. She does not tell us what caused her to collapse but explains her soul slipped out of her body as though made of satin. She went to a place she instinctively knew was home and met some people there.

The guides thought it was very funny that I was there. It was as if I was trying to get out of this life experience before my time. No part of me wanted to return to this life. This may sound arrogant, but I thought this life was beneath me. It felt like I was playing a kindergarten game, when I was much more intelligent than that.

I returned with the realization that no one is better than anyone else. Everyone is here for a purpose. I had decided to make this journey but hadn't realized how hard it would be. I tried to tell them that I had changed my mind. I really didn't want to do this life. My friends over there laughed and thought this was very funny. Then I knew there was no way to change it. I had to see it through. I was shown my future and how it would be. I remember feeling dread of what was to come. My friends showed no sympathy for me. They just found it very amusing.

As I returned to my body, the limitations of life engulfed me. The senses, tasting, feeling, hearing, and smelling were nothing compared to the freedom of having no body. I could feel how trapped I was. It felt like I had been thrown into jail. My spirit was imprisoned in this gross body. With this attitude, it was hard to adjust. Clearly, I was not happy here. Still, I knew, that I had to play this one out, and I am. But now, through other experiences, I have come to value this life. I'm not aware of anyone trying to show me anything. It was simply my own rebellious spirit trying to sneak out of this vow. But there can be no hiding on the other side.

Michelle shared part of her experience in chapter 9 on Knowledge. Immediately after she was hit by a car, she found herself talking to a beautiful being of light. Michelle had no idea how she got there. A guide explained she had been in an accident. While in the other dimension, she had a life review and was filled with an amazing understanding of how it all works before she thought about returning.

My children came to my mind. As if I turned one last time to look at my life, I thought of my children. I saw my twin sons' lives and felt that all was good for them. They would enjoy their lives. They were going to have a good life. I was filled with such love and compassion for them. I saw my daughter's life. It was going to be difficult, and she would need someone. She would go through some terrible times. I was afraid for her and guilt for not being there when she needed me.

I understood that whatever happened in life, we were okay because it was temporary. I also realized that I was still attached to this life and not finished yet.

Then the two beautiful Men and I were traveling through the cosmos, and I saw the splendor of the Earth and stunning beauty of the infinite universe. Total peace embraced me. Suddenly, without warning, I felt unbearable pain, and everything seemed so thick. I was back in this life in the emergency room. I wasn't able to remember my name or where I was.

Hannah's feelings at having returned to this physical life are not unusual. Many people become depressed, angry, and confused when they return. She died twice during a cesarean section while giving birth to her second child. Once she saw her daughter, she simply let go and died. Then, she found herself in a beautiful garden surrounded by peace and a gentle spirit by her side.

It seemed like hours later I awoke back in my body. It was so sudden I had no idea how this had happened. The doctors rushed in and I was not happy that they had brought me back. I did not want to return, ever. I just wanted to stay there in peace, happiness, and love. Not back here, on Earth. I screamed, bellowed and cried. Later, they told me that this was a normal reaction for somebody who had been dead.

They told my now ex-husband that I had died. I think I was brought back by something else, not the doctors. They had given up on me and were ready to send me to the morgue. Ten minutes after I had been declared dead, I came back.

Maria was visiting Bulgaria and had a miscarriage. Toward the beginning of the operation, she felt the anesthetic burning as it went into her system. She thought it was too strong but before she could say anything she died. Maria felt herself dying and became very angry with the doctors. After a short stay in the light and the beautiful feelings of love and peace, she reluctantly returned.

Then I decided that it wasn't so bad there. I didn't want to return to Earth. No not ever again. I couldn't see why I should go back. Everything there was so materialistic. It felt like I needed to fight so hard for results. It just seemed like a lot of work for nothing. On the other side, I could move as I wanted—wherever I want.

While I was blissfully enjoying this new situation of total freedom and Love, a force dragged me back into my body.

Karen's information has been saved until now because it is different from most other reports on returning. She was killed in a serious car accident and immediately joined by other spirits. Seven months earlier, she had given birth to a boy, and unlike others, she did not want to stay in the afterlife because she wanted to raise her son. However, it was quite a chore for her to come back.

With each moment I became lighter as I went to my destination. Fear and panic gripped me. No, I cried, I can't be dead. My thoughts were totally on my seven-month-old son. I was worried about what would happen for him. His father had no idea how to take care of him. I did not want my in-laws to raise him. No, oh no, that was all wrong.

An embrace of love surrounded me, and my guides calmed me. They showed me that my baby and the rest of my family would be okay following my death. Al this time I was feeling lighter and lighter. But wait. My son. I couldn't leave him! Babies need their mommies. I needed to be the one to raise him. I was not able to let go. My guides showed me so much patience—so much love.

My guides explained that I was feeling this way because I was still attached to my human life. Once that wore off I would feel as light as air, filled with absolute happiness, and extreme love. They strived to help me to discard my human weight. The wonderful feelings were so overpowering, they seemed to pull me in stronger and stronger. Yet the connection to my son was too strong and my thoughts of him made me feel heavy again. The mere thought of him growing up without a mother was unbearable even though I knew others would mother him.

There were other lessons learned from the constant patience of the guides transitioning me to accept the situation. Sometimes, I was hysterical and moments later, I was calm and serene. When I felt close to accepting my death, I would have a resurgence of sorrow, pain, longing for my son, and the life I lost. I was not able let go of my human life. My guides worked so hard. They never gave up or became discouraged. I was astonished at the amount of patience and love they exuded. Finally, a higher spirit calmed my hysteria. This being enveloped me in pure love. My guides were told to allow me to return. They begged for more time. But they were told that my spirit was not going to rest. It was best to let me return to my life and settle my soul. I would have to learn further lessons. Although my pleading gained my return for the time being. I realized that my return disrupted the lessons my friends and family were to have in this lifetime. But they would have to learn them at a later date.

I was taken back to the site of the accident. Moments before I reentered my body, I was told that when the children were older, it would be time for me to come home for good. I accepted it immediately but had second thoughts. What did they mean by older? Was it a few years older? When they were teenagers? Would I see them marry and have children? This was a difficult phase to deal with immediately after the accident. While I had a life with my son again. I needed to spend it right because I had no idea how long I had with them.

There is no clear explanation why some people are given a choice while others are not. Still, others are returned without discussion. The only clarification given is things that need to be done, and they can return once they are completed.

21

The World and Us

Education is the great liberator that opens us to the amazement of each other, nature, and the big and small universes. It offers gifts of comprehension to the mysteries of life. And provides greater levels of freedom, exploration, and understanding of those questions we perpetually ask. Knowledge also assists us with problem-solving, plus we are not as easily victims of scams and cons.

The primary job of a country's leader is the betterment of the land for its residents. Sadly, too often, it has been used to gain power and control over its citizens and neighbors, where possible, and to feed the hubris of its leader. These leaders have sought to lock up the residents' minds and spoon-feed them only with what they want them to know. Frequently, this is coupled with minimal living conditions, thus giving the leaders greater control over their vassals.

Over a prolonged time, these conditions caused the people to become naïve, childlike, and open to superstitions and false stories by the authorities. Those unsatisfied with the information they are fed seek other explanations, often at great peril. Others erroneously invent rationales to explain what they don't understand. Numerous religions and philosophies have developed over the centuries with offers of explanations of things beyond our control.

Today, technological advances gallop through our lives at top speed and bring remarkable advancements. The techno-world stretches its fingers out to touch everywhere with the promise of a new and freer life. The world is becoming smaller and smaller, and the internet is connecting people like never before.

Dr. Michio Kaku proposes an interesting concept.[30] He postulates that if the universe had a scale of the developmental levels of all the planets from one to ten, Earth would be at a zero. He feels we are only getting ready to climb out of the basement as we approach level one about one hundred years from now. Dr. Kaku thinks our world is presently struggling with growing pains and is on the brink of wonderful new changes that will take us in entirely new directions—that is, he adds, if we can survive the present stage. We can either wipe ourselves off the face of the Earth through various methods or grow to the next level. The choice is ours.

Below are some NDErs who brought back intelligence about our relationships with ourselves and others and how those could impact the world.

Nevie died as a young teen when she decided she was old enough to drink and proceeded to gulp down a water tumbler filled with liquor. Her body could not handle the shock of that much alcohol, and she died. This is a part of her experience.

I understood that death is a normal process that all humans must go through. Death is only a step in an ongoing procession of being. The developmental stage in learning how to love. While concurrently avoiding the traps and pitfalls of our fragile human makeup. We are persuaded to get back up after our falls, recover, and move forward to a destiny we had a part in creating.

I now comprehend that we are active participants in our destiny through the choices we make. at every moment. We aren't puppets of clay providing entertainment for the gods.

Teri was in a vehicle accident and died from her injuries. While she also experienced the love, they all speak of, the understanding she returned with and what she did with it are lessons we could all use for a peaceful world.

Because she had experienced a very negative life, Teri slung her anger over her shoulder and carried it with her wherever she went.

Wherever we go we take ourselves with us. Our awareness must change for us to experience the higher frequencies of love, peace, joy, and tranquility. Within we truly become whatever we want to be.

I knew that I had to find a way to raise my vibration and become more loving if I, in turn, wanted to know this indescribable love on a permanent basis. With these insights I recognized more about how things worked. I wanted to do better, not out of fear but because of love.

Energetically, love is the link we all have with the highest vibration. When love is the foundation of our actions, we create empowering energy that raises our understanding to higher levels. Our fears, anger, and negative emotions are damaging energies. They break down communication between ourselves and our growth toward higher realms where joy, peace, and tranquility can be experienced.

With the resolve to bring the love she experienced with her to Earth, Teri immediately found her "buttons" were still easily pushed. I admire and respect the tenacity she has shown in her resolve. Teri tells us of the journey she went on, and, in the end, she found love in her life for everyone.

I was determined to keep my NDE to myself. I would keep working on myself until I had changed myself. Twenty-five years later with persistent dedication to that purpose I found a way. Slowly, I made progress over the years. I had some very deep-seated wounds and anger that no amount of willpower and determination seemed to help.

My experience was the stimulus that transformed me into a utterly different person. After years of trial and error and scientific discoveries, I finally improved the ability to feel love for everyone, no matter what.

That is a place of power that I now use to help others make positive changes in their lives and in their world. Now, I have replaced the feeling anger over corruption and dishonesty heard about in the news. Instead, I create warm, loving thoughts and feelings and project that energy into the situation. The love doesn't always come instant, but I get there 100 percent of the time.

My goal is now to feel unconditional love all the time. I'm still working on shifting my frequency to where I can feel the warmth of love in my heart on any occasion. Now, I'm working on getting there quicker and staying there longer. I want to do it without being pulled back into the energy that creates the challenges of everyday life.

Marta was not a happy person at the time of her death. Although there is no information about what caused her death, she returned with some valuable information.

We entail a single being with all creation. Our Earthly eyes provide a way through which Source can recognize and be conscious of Self. Everything we think, feel, and do stays imprinted in the universe. We experience this life to improve ourselves. We come to understand through humility about all that surrounds us. And to teach these lessons to others. Being is focused on two aspects: love and service.

Anita Moorjani's experience was very deep and enlightening. Through discussions with friends on NDERF, Anita showed us that, through the connection of Oneness, not only are all connected, but aspects of our existence intermingle in one clear understanding.

Incredible clarity, like a bright, royal-purple shard, helped me realize that everything that is done here in the physical from limitations.

Since my NDE my perception of the world is that there's no such thing as sinners or fallen people. Erroneously, we assess ourselves against an unrealistic paradigm of perfection and we will never succeed. In addition, we also assess others using the same ideological model, and predictably, everyone falls short. With this model to follow, we struggle, with loving ourselves and others. Then we become angry, aggressive, and violent toward ourselves and others.

Armed with the knowledge from my NDE, I recognized that everyone is already perfectly magnificent, but they don't know it. We all are worthy, deserving, and lovable, without exception. When we realize our magnificence and see our soul as God (which is who we truly are), only then will we recognize God within all others.

Hitler was just as magnificent as Mother Teresa. But he had no awareness of it. At death he would probably have realized it. But if he had known of his radiant glory in life, he would have behaved very differently because he would have acknowledged the God within others.

The Greek philosopher Epictetus (55—135CE said, "You are a primary existence. You are a distinct portion of the essence of God and contain a certain part of Him in yourself. Why, then, are you ignorant of your noble birth? You carry God about within you, poor wretch, and know nothing of it."

Several NDErs asked for information on the future. They were concerned about the strife worldwide and wanted to know if we would ever live peacefully. A few reported seeing visions of war and increased disasters, after which there would be peace, but they were in the minority. Indeed, very few people brought back reports of a specific future for our world; most simply returned with knowledge of their own destiny and that of their loved ones. In contradiction, the occasional person said that because time did not actually exist, neither did the future or the past. Still, others returned after seeing what lies ahead for the world, but they were not allowed to bring back understanding with them.

Many who asked about the future did not get the answer they hoped for. They were repeatedly told that everything was as it should be and not to worry. These answers leave giant questions. Are the violence, poverty, and cruelty we now see leading us to a time of peace? What about the astonishing increase in natural disasters around the world? Could it be the brink of a remarkable new level of existence, and everything truly is as it should be? Or will we continue to spiral down to oblivion? Only time will bring an answer to these questions.

Take heart, my friends, there may be an increase in violence and natural disasters in the world. But there is also an increase in the number of people who are having near-dearth experiences, spiritually transformative experiences and other spiritual events that are having an impact on the consciousness of everyone, everywhere. I believe that twenty years from now, the world will be a much kinder, caring place. One spiritual experience at a time.

22

Healing

Miraculous healings happen, and there are a bunch of people who would love to tell you about theirs. As if a giant hocus-pokus swept over them, they returned well on the way to good health. In this chapter, we discover it is through our merger with the Source that the marvelous has become a reality. Miseries, pains, and sicknesses have developed from our forgetfulness of this association. While traveling in the realm of death, NDErs have been put through a spiritual Laundromat and returned with their bodies, minds, and souls healed.

Now we understand no evil lurks in the background, waiting to crush us in hell here or in the afterlife. In the chapter on Evil, we saw it is not possible because hell and the Devil are human constructions, pure fantasy. How can evil and hell exist if we are closer than the glowing heart to the Loving Light? If we are, as reported, completely One with the Source, where are our ills coming from? Have we listened too closely to the threats of sin and damnation? We have conjured up a brew of pain to match what we feel we deserve or inadvertently ask for.

Amazing healings happened during people's NDEs. Some were consciously aware of the process and took an active role in bringing about their wellness. Others returned healed of whatever took them into death with no idea how it was done. Still, others were not cured but sent back to deal with the illness or injuries in the best way they could.

Here are some accounts of people who experienced healing.

Anita Moorjani's NDE gives us a clear explanation of her healing, the marvel of our being, and how that relates to being cured. Her jaw-dropping story is one of love, hope, and encouragement to each of us. Once more, she shares her wonderful wisdom with us and how it relates to healing. Anita's own words from her book, *Dying to be Me,* are so eloquent that I have left them here for you.

"I want to stress this next realization so that each person will know the importance of it. If we each individually recognized the magnificent, fantastic, marvelous soul they were, then it would reflect itself in their lives.

In the afterlife, no restricting boxes existed. I was free to be all that I wanted to be in whichever life I chose. I was immersed in a place of freedom and abundant limitlessness. It was like nothing was real, yet, simultaneously, every possibility existed.

"Along with the amazing awareness of freedom came the realization that even the cancer I had struggled with for so long was an illusion. It, too, had been crafted, shaped, and honed by the thoughts and beliefs of myself and my world. In turn, I produced this horrid disease for myself. In this new dimension, I became sensitive to the fact that suffering was brought about by human thoughts and beliefs. In response, this, too, I had accepted into my reality.

"The love, oh the glorious, inexpressible love—I was overwhelmed as I stood under the fountain and bathed in the wonder of what was coming to me. It was from this Source that I knew how powerful I was. As an astounding gift, I became aware of my own magnificence. The beauty of my reality was beyond my ability to comprehend. As if with a great eureka, I suddenly understood that it was me I hadn't forgiven, not other people. It was me whom I judged harshly. I did not love myself enough. My self-loathing had nothing to do with anyone else. No blame, no guilt could be given to another.

"A thought of beauty, opportunity, and encouragement shot through me like a lightning bolt. Heaven is not a place, I realized; it is a state from within. Heaven is a state of mind. Heaven is right here inside of me. In reality, there is no heaven or hell "out there" on the other side of the veil. It is all here with us now. More accurately, it is within ourselves. When I discovered I carry it within me wherever I am, no matter what side of death's veil I was on, I chose to come back.

"I knew that not only was the cancer an illusion, but even this body I resided in and this whole three-dimensional reality was an illusion. I knew with pure certainty that the body was nothing more than a pod or casing in which to accommodate the soul. I had finally found the answers to my life-long quest. The answers were not anywhere outside; they were right here inside my own being. I was my own answer. I had created my cancer! And I could also produce my own healing!"

Anita's experience is the most vivid in talking about the reality of our being; "It was like nothing was real and yet, simultaneously, every possibility existed." This comment at the beginning of her report says it all. Every possibility exists for each one of us to choose. In her book, *Dying to be Me,* Anita talks of an infinitely vast warehouse where every thought and dream is available. But we, in our limited vision, only see one or two corners of what is accessible.

Geralyn was thirteen when she was diagnosed with Burkett's lymphoma, a form of cancer. She was given only a 1 percent chance of survival, and her parents were told to begin to plan arrangements for her death. By the time she died, the disease had ravished her body and taken over her organs; the spleen, liver, and intestines were filled with tumors. Another large tumor was blocking her bowels, and she was rushed into surgery, where she died.

Unexpectedly, a giant hand came toward me. I can't express its size. Everything in that dimension was more than words could express. Yet, it was a non-threatening hand, that glowed with an astonishing light. That's when I heard a soft, yet authoritative voice telling me to go back because I had a lot of work I still needed to do.

In that moment, I knew that I was healed. The doctors and nurses were astounded to find the tumors gone after only one chemo treatment. And that action was done against my will. Because I was too young for them to acknowledge my protest. Now, thirty-seven years later, I'm still here.

Rick has another amazing story of healing. He is the man who was alone in the wilderness when he fell down an eighty-foot cliff and landed on the boulders below. During his death experience, he was also told to return. Like most NDErs, he did not want to come back but knew he had no choice because he needed to learn to be more giving. Just before he was sent back, a disembodied voice gave him some important information.

The voice warned me that the doctors would want to operate on me. It was stressed to not let this happen! If they proceeded, I would never walk again. I must be patient and I will recover from all the damage.

Two doctors introduced themselves and explained that they were my attending physicians. They explained that I needed surgery as soon as possible. Then, the warning I had heard before came back to me: Don't let them operate, or you won't ever walk again. Complete understanding filled me.

When I refused the surgery, the doctors were dismayed. Then came lecture after lecture but I resisted as instructed. Finally, they turned away and said OK if you don't ever want to walk again, that's up to you, and they left.

Time lingered with nothing happening. Then one morning, a few months later, my feet tingled! I was overcome with joy. I rang for the nurse and told her I wanted to walk. She stared at me in disbelief and said we would see if that was possible. Of course, I knew it was. The next day my doctor stopped by. "So, you think you can walk?"

"Yes," I replied.

"Well, we will see."

A few hours later, they took me to the physical therapy room. They carried me to the parallel bars and raised me to a vertical position. The nurse arranged me in front of the bars and I gripped them tightly, placed my feet firmly on the floor, and began walking. The nurses were astounded. My doctor was even more shocked when he had me x-rayed and found nothing pressing on my spinal nerves. I use his quote: "This is not normal. It seems a higher power has done for you what we were going to try and correct with surgery. I have never seen anything like this before!"

Randi was an adolescent who awoke one morning too sick to move or to respond to his mother's call to get ready for school. After repeated tries, he finally got his mother's attention. He was taken to the hospital, where it was learned that he had spinal meningitis. Randi tells us that there were fourteen others in his school who contracted the disease, and he was the only one who survived. It appears his survival almost did not happen as he slipped into a coma and found himself in darkness.

Although I was surrounded in darkness it didn't last a long time. I felt myself moving and then there were thousands of colors in front of me like a very colorful aurora borealis. Then, strangely, one of the colors noticed me and came up to me and lifted me. I became a part of the stream of colors and felt myself moving along the rainbow as if it were solid.

The figure of my deceased uncle appeared before me. He explained that I was not where I was supposed to be. I looked around and there was a very bright light in the distance and to my right. He told me that was heaven and held out his hand for me to hold it. When I grasped it, pictures of things formed in my mind. Suddenly my mind was filled with knowledge. In the short split second that he touched my hand, I knew all knowledge there was to know or would be known, except one thing. He told me that I had to make a choice. I could go into the light and heaven. If that's what I chose he would guide me there. Or I could go back, as it was too early and not my time.

Seconds later, I was throwing the covers off my head. I was in the hospital surrounded by deceased people in the hospital morgue. That's when I heard a blood-curdling scream and saw someone run out of the room. A few minutes later, a group of people came into the room to attend to me.

They did tests for meningitis but couldn't find it in my body. The doctors asked me to stay in the hospital for an further two weeks for tests and to find out what had happened and why I was alive.

On the day I was leaving my doctor said that my case was going to be placed in the annals of medicine.

Anthony talked to us in the chapter on Returning about the joy he has found in life. He had been dead for over thirty minutes when he returned. As mentioned earlier, he was treated by the best neurosurgeons. Yet, he suffered major head trauma, and the doctors did not hold out much hope for him.

Although the doctors had removed a third of my brain, after less than six months of rehabilitation, there are no neural, cognitive, emotional, or psychological deficits. They had told my family I wouldn't live out the week. That, if I ever came out of my coma, I would be like a vegetable or comatose at best. They thought I'd be lucky to survive and would require long-term care for the rest of my life. They even helped my family choose nursing homes in the area. If you met me today, you could not tell I was in such a horrific accident.

Lynn K Russell

Medically there is no way to explain my survival. It can all be verified by several doctors, specialists, surgeons, etc. They told me there is no medical explanation for why I was recovering so remarkably. They added that after what I'd been through, the only explanation was divine intervention."

It is fantastic and astounding to realize these people, through their connection with the wonder of their authentic Being, were able to bring about healing. When we understand our Oneness with the power of the Loving Light, we can see how we are right there, like a kid with a computer game, taking an active role in our healing.

Alas, there were far more people who continued to struggle with their illness upon returning from their NDE. This lack of recovery does not mean there was something wrong with them or their soul, nor does it mean they were being punished. Could we punish our hand or foot for its actions? Possibly, these disabilities were a part of the soul's contract before coming into the physical universe. As we have learned, once the agreement is made, it is impossible to break.

Those who suffer are not bad, blamed, or cheated; their suffering has nothing to do with karma or paying back for some past sin. It simply means there are things we still need to learn. While we do not have all the answers, it is important to keep the reality of our being in mind when we think about healing miracles.

23

Creation

We may smile at a young child examining a caterpillar or a flower in fascination. Yet, adults take a page from this book as our inquisitiveness never dies. We continue to peek under rocks, look behind things tucked in the corner, and open dusty closets in the exploration of answers. From the birth of humanity, our incredible curiosity has peppered the universe and beyond in search of knowledge and understanding. The mere fact of our existence shoots out reams of queries that have baffled us since we first stood on two legs.

Why are we? What purpose does our existence serve? To what or whom beyond ourselves does our existence have relevance? How did it all begin? These questions have become precious gems of conjecture for philosophers and theologians throughout the centuries and provide us with a string of sparkling speculations. Today's great thinkers are putting a whole new slant on the question of our existence.

NDErs tell us, from the most minuscule particle of the quantum world to the vast expanse of the multiverse, that all we know is constructed from Love. Love is a momentous power that permeates everything and brings about micro and macro existence. In the chapter on Love, we talked about the essence of the Source is love. At that level, it is not an emotion but a primary element of existence.

The Source not only creates because it wants but because there is no other choice. The Loving, Creative Energy is a vast power greater than the Big Bang. In ecstatic joy, it produces because the Love Force that is the essence of Its being compels nothing less.

Further, because we are one with the Creator, we also take an active role in creating all we know here in this world, throughout the whole universe, and beyond. The soul of us that is living this life never truly left the Source. We are, right this second, not only a soul living in a body; we are also existing within the Source and perpetually creating.

Allow a few people to share with you what they learned.

Here is **Debi-Sue** once again sharing more of her amazing NDE with us. She gives us a marvelous vision of the creative process as the universe is perpetually formed.

Imagine a large, round, globe-shaped zinnia with a deep golden center made up of countless petite petals. These glorious petals come from within the Light Being. As each miniature petal moves outward the center is perpetually being refilled and multiplied. Infinitely being created from the power of Love within the Being of Light. Creation, as love made real, manifested.

Each living thing was created through the power of Divine Love. The radiating love, like the sunbeams on a hot summer day, touches everything in the universe. This was the intimate detail the Loving Light shared with me.

James shared parts of his experience in chapter 13 on Time. After his second NDE, he explains his understanding of our reality.

It looked something like a sun or a planet of light until I got close enough to see details. Suddenly, I realized that all was revealed, and even that is a poor description of what was conveyed. I became aware of billions and billions of bits of light spiraling to and from this enormous "Body of Light." It was a visual description of what we call "God." We quite literally are God since this Being of Light cannot be whole *without all its parts or bits of light.*

Once more, **Hafur** shares her sense of creation with us:

The Source is eternally creating into infinity. One creation is the procedure of conscious love. One learns a skill by doing it. That's why this time-based earthly human illusory creation exists as though it were a template within another template and within another... multidimensionally until we wake up to our reality.

Dan was undergoing open heart surgery when he had his amazing experience. We are very fortunate he came back and shared his experience with us.

Creation appeared before me, and I saw all of Creation as in a crystal ball. A Being of exquisite majesty was wrapped around Creation as if it grew from its body.

I looked beneath Creation and saw that every living thing was an expression of this Being. All was connected to this Being, inseparable, and One. Included every person, plants, animals, insects, and even microbes. All derived its existence from that resplendent Source.

The recognition was that everything is interconnected always and forever. Including the largest galactic cluster spiraling around the core of Creation to the most petite quantum fluctuation. All was revealed. How everyone and everything has a place and a reason.

Angela was in the hospital for an unknown illness and simply stopped breathing. During her time in the other dimension, she knew almost immediately she was going to come back to this life. However, two of her guides wanted her to learn some lessons before her return.

They asked me to walk through a doorway. I was a bit confused because I didn't understand what they wanted. But I trusted them, so, although confused, I walked through and felt absolutely nothing different. I told them nothing happened.

They asked me to do it again with shoes. I looked down and saw I had legs and was wearing bright red sneakers. It seems strange now, but I had never considered my "body." I had only considered what I saw beyond it.

A second time I walked through the doorway and again felt nothing. and told them so. They said to look at my feet. Strangely, the shoes remained on the other side of the threshold. They asked what I had learned. Quickly, I told them that we couldn't bring material things with us when we die. I felt pleased with my answer, although there seemed to be more because my answer had seemed obvious.

They keep on and again pertaining to the secondary question, "...And?" Then words sprang from my mouth like they'd always been there, just out of my understanding. Instantly, I realized that I felt nothing when I walked through the door because I hadn't changed. My location had. The shoes weren't a part of me. I told them that we don't change when we die. We are always butterflies. We just move on to a different location." Understanding what I said reverberated into my soul.

They asked me to watch something. In the distance, I saw something growing. Was I moving closer or was it growing bigger. Eventually, I could see little beings wrapping ribbons of light around a central something. The closer I got, the more I could see. I recognized all the things that are part of the universe. There were cats, mountains, trees, rivers, people, stars—so many things simmering together. It was akin to a soup of wholeness. Each element was thought out in detail in their bubbles only to pop and join everything else.

I cannot begin to tell you the delight—euphoria—I felt as I watched this happen. It was the greatest happiness I'd ever felt in my life. They asked me what I was seeing, and I said (as though I had no doubt at all), "Creation."

They asked me to tell them what I had learned. I joyfully told them that everything is everything else.

They then again asked with a simple "...And?" I was infused with knowledge I never knew I possessed. I easily answered that everyone matters to everything." It was fascinating to hear answers I didn't know I knew come from my lips.

They said, "Good."

Nanci reacted quite badly to a needle-location procedure to identify the place where a surgeon needed to cut to remove some potentially cancerous lesions.

Though the tunnel was as real as anything experienced on Earth, I realized without a doubt that I wasn't in a tunnel. Its appearance didn't fool me. With that realization, I was inundated with knowledge about manifesting our reality.

I understood that we are perpetually manifesting our physical reality simply by virtue of our thoughts. The reason we become fooled into believing this life is real is because of our limited human senses.

You can imagine how astonished I was by this information. And I believed it without a doubt. To test it out, I experimented with intentionally consciously manifesting some tests to its truth. I demonstrated to myself that we do truly have the ability to determine what we perceive to be our physical reality. We do this by focusing our attention and intention on doing so."

We are left with a question: who creates whom? Given what we have learned so far, we realize that we are indivisible from the Creator; thus, we actively participate in all we see and know, including ourselves. Some may feel uncomfortable acknowledging their role as creators. Like Atlas, try to hold up the world and struggle with the overpowering responsibility. There are no Cinderellas here; one meager soul does not do all the work. We are the great Loving Light experiencing life. If we allow ourselves to look at the larger picture, we see the beauty of it, and we are in awe.

24

Slight of Mind

Seekers of spiritual truth have been delighted as the truth of our Oneness with all that exists spreads throughout the world. Some may see our relationship like drops of water from an ocean or needles on a giant pine tree. Not so. We *are* the tree and all its parts, and as Rumi says, we are the whole ocean. It is not enough to have this understanding in our heads; we must also know it in our hearts and demonstrate it as a part of our daily lives. It is impossible to comprehend the Oneness and then treat another person, place, or thing with anything less than the love and respect they or it deserves. The awareness of the truth of our being must be as close to us as our beating hearts and the blood pumping through our bodies.

With the certainty of our existence, we need to *know* we are far more than just connected to one another by an invisible cord. It is imperative we realize we *are* the abused women everywhere; we are the starving people in developing countries, the untouchables in India, and the homeless people in the inner cities of the world. In precisely the same way, we are multimillionaires living in luxury, and simultaneously, the insane leaders of countries raining war and destruction upon the innocent.

The Oneness we speak of is much deeper and spreads further than most of us have judged. We are One with the universe, all that exists. That planet on the other side of the

universe with the strange life forms is as much One with yo
as your own baby toenail.

One means one and only one, and there is nothing more
no pieces or parts, only Oneness. The second we see ourselve
as separate from our Source, we are the ones creating th
illusion of separation. In truth, we cannot ever be apart fror
the Creative Force. It is our truth.

The ego personalities we carry around during ou
lifetimes are nothing more than temporary passports into life
Whether good or bad, our egos are simply illusions we hav
created as useful tools to serve us while we dream our physica
existence into being. The personality may be loving or hatefu
yet at the spirit level, they remain as illusionary as
magician's conjuring.

We truly are souls experiencing human existence. Ou
egos or personalities do not live this life; that is the soul. It i
the soul that gives the illusion of a body with a heart and bloo
rushing through our veins and arteries. The soul keeps ou
lungs working, our cells dividing, and our organs doing wha
they should. And, regardless of our developed egos, it is th
soul living this life, not the ego.

Our souls give us the illusion of sitting down to eat
laughing with friends, and crying over our pains. The sou
plays sports, gives birth, and goes to work every day. And ou
souls are the Creator experiencing life in this physical form
There is no separation, and never was. It matters not that w
relate more to our ego personalities. There has never been
time when we were separated from Source.

At eighteen, I was an unemployed hairdresser desperat
to find a job and willing to do almost anything to put some
bucks in my pocket. Being the brave individual I was,

applied for a job to do the hair of corpses. (I had never seen a corpse in my life). On the day of my first job, I nervously followed the funeral director to the room where the body waited and was completely shocked by the mannequin lying on the table. I expected to see a woman caught in a deep sleep. But that object lying there was nothing. Once, there had been a person in that body. A woman who spent time with her family, worked, laughed, and cried. Now, there was no person; nothing to even indicate that life had ever existed there. A life-like doll lay on the metal table and nothing more.

At that moment, I discovered the soul. The instant the soul had left that body, she stopped being a human being. Her soul no longer ran the show. The lights were turned off, the doors had been locked, and nothing was left.

The ego did not—indeed could not—jump in to carry on in place of the soul. That wasn't possible. The soul had lived this woman's life. It's the soul that's operating our bodies as well. And when the job is done, the soul packs up its lunch pail, punches the time clock, and leaves to go home.

Those who returned from death tell us that our physical existence is an illusion. It's a dream brought about by Source, experiencing Self. Like Pinocchio, we dreamed of being real, and—abracadabra—we gave ourselves the gift of human life.

Hafur returned with a list of new realizations she had gained while in the other dimension. The things on this list are so much a part of our reality and the illusions of our existence.

There is no god beyond ourselves. More exactly, we are in everything, and everything is Source, as is life itself.

Source is everything and nothing simultaneously. The universe is infinite, absolute consciousness. We reside in a mental dream that's perpetually being created as a dynamic of consciousness that recognizes itself and recreates itself through the illusion of physical life.

Our life is the juncture of nothingness, where the void or nothingness of the universe develops aware of itself. It's extremely hard to explain such a foreign, abstract concept. All we know originates from universal mind projected into images and events that interact with lucid consciousness as an experience. This total existence is a part of the limitlessness of that which is real on every level of existence. We invent and separate into pieces so that our earthly mind can decipher it despite the brain's limitations.

There is only one law: LIFE. Death does not exist.

The universe is part of a necessary game of life itself. We come to understanding to the degree that we live by true love—unconditional and universal. The closer we are to realizing what life truly is the greater the happiness and perfect wisdom.

How can something be everything and nothing at the same time? Source is the force of all concepts. Without God, nothing exists. Throughout the book, we have learned that, through love-power, all we know becomes. However, in reality, nothing exists. All creation is an illusion. And the only entity in existence is Source

Rev. Juliet also tells of her concept of the illusion of our understanding. A short time later, she departed this life, and part of her message reflects this.

How blessed it is, to realize that as souls, we are a part of all creation and share in the actual creative process!

I was told that the world was an illusion and not to identify with it or be involved—to be in it but not of it—as I was only passing through.

Love is always the dominant force, no matter how things may appear in this world of duality and illusion. It is merely a hologram—created by the collective consciousness—for the sake of growth and evolution.

Anita Moorjani shares her understanding about the illusion of our existence.

The world, universe, and life itself are an incredible game of pretend. Yes, that's right...the universe and this life we think we are living has become an <u>amazing trick of the mind.</u> Each of us creates our existence, circumstances, and universe. This is done this how much love we have.

It is as simple and difficult as we make it. In the physical world, we imagine we are solid. Before my NDE, if anyone had asked me if we are solid, I would have wondered what they were talking about. Fundamentally, I would have agreed that we're solid. I would have held out my arm to show them how solid it was. "See, I'm solid. I feel solid, look solid. Everything about me is solid. So, what's your point?"

Now, I can tell you with deep conviction, that we are not solid. Indeed, we aren't even here. In truth, our reality is a colossal power that created this world. This energy that is us and everything is actually cosmic energy that has been condensed and compacted into creations of three-dimensional images—substance we relate to as whole.

I knew that not only was my cancer an illusion, but even this body I resided in and this whole three-dimensional reality was an illusion. I knew with pure certainty that the body was a pod or casing to contain the soul.

It is interesting to note quantum physics agrees with Anita's point of not being solid. We will look at this aspect in the last chapter when we look at life and death from a scientific point of view.

Larry had a heart attack while driving his wife to work one morning. After she took over the driving, he passed out and started flopping around in the truck like a fish out of water. His wife understandably panicked and drove him straight to the hospital. After Larry's NDE, he came back scratching his head and wondering at the marvel of his realization.

Everything I see here is not real anymore. Nothing I see is real. What I saw over there was real. This life is an imitation. I saw the "real McCoy." I take things more seriously and listen more, but I don't take it for truth. It's not as real as what I saw. I still listen and watch the servers pour my coffee, but it's not real. Whenever I pick up a magazine or vatch TV, I know it is material, but it's not real. What I saw vas real. This is not real.

*You're going to go to a nice place after death, a real place. You're going to be in the **real** world. Where you're at now is temporary. You will go to the **real** world.*

This is man-made, human made. The other side is not manufactured. That's real.

Nancy visited us above when she shared her return with us. Now, she explains her thoughts on illusions this way:

The degree of closeness revealed that we aren't separate individuals at all. This experience is an illusion and a wonderful gift. In fact, we are part of Source's self-awareness. That reality should remove all doubt about the outcome of life and how it should be lived. Our usual level of consciousness while awake is just one tiny segment of the Consciousness I experienced during the NDE. It's as though we have forgotten who we really are. More importantly, the consciousness we experience while in the body operates at such a slow vibration that we perceive our human lives as reality. When it is really an illusion. The intensity of Source's love, understanding, and willingness to allow us to continue the illusion of separation astounds me.

More and more lately, we are seeing quotes and memes telling us to be careful of what we think. What does this mean?

Everything in our lives stems from thought. Everything. When we see, we first get a signal in our brains that tells us there is something we want to see. This happens so quickly and constantly that we don't give it any attention. If we want to move our hands, walk, or eat, each begins within the brain. This includes our senses, taste, hearing, feeling (both physical and emotional), and smell. Each one of these demands begins in the mind through thought.

Thoughts are enormously powerful things. They are the creative force in the universe. Because we are the Source, we are that universal consciousness that is perpetually overflowing like a multi-petaled flower.

25

Your Reality

In our search for answers, we have developed education in language, mathematics, philosophy, psychology, and much more. Plus, there is a mountain more that we have yet to discover. We can click on the NASA website and marvel at the splendor of nebulae spilling their luminosity so far across the cosmos that it would easily swallow our whole solar system in one vast, smothering gulp.

Today, responses to another area of eternal questions come to us from an unlikely source. Astonishing information is coming from those who have died and returned to life to share their new knowledge and assure us of our true reality. On a warm and sunny day, as we watch the birds soar on the breeze, we are up there with them. We have wings that can take us distances beyond our imagination.

Let's take a journey through a mind exploration. Imagine a time before the beginning when creation has yet to happen. There is no space or time, no universes. All that exists is an eternal nothingness.

Now, suppose within that emptiness dwells a single lone consciousness. An aware eternal being that always has been and always will be, with no beginning and no end. Our sole entity is encircled by nothingness. There are no stars, galaxies, or multi-universes, and no life anywhere. Not so much as a nanoparticle floating past in the void. There is no other existence to interact with; there is only our eternal being and nothingness.

Further, imagine this entity possesses intelligence beyond any ceiling we can conger. It is a colossal intellect that surpasses anything we can conceive.

If this scenario were possible, then existence would have no value. Our imaginary being would be blind, deaf, and dumb, for there would be nothing to see, hear, smell, touch, or taste. And although it has the capacity for thought, that ability would not matter because there is nothing to think about except the Self.

But what is that? How would the entity know itself without others? How can it know 'me' without a 'you?' Would our entity even know it exists? With nothing to relate to, how would it identify its own existence? And even if it somehow did recognize its being, without anything to connect that realization to, it would exist in perpetual lonely nothingness. If such a situation could exist, the entity's intelligence would drive it to do something—anything—to recognize its own existence and know itself. It would take less than a nanosecond before creation would begin.

This scenario is not too far off the mark. If we accept the information NDErs have brought back, then we know there is only one Creative Force. Some of our NDE friends tell us they were taken back to the beginning of creation and nothingness.

Our imagined story needs a bit more before it is finished. We must consider the fabrication process itself. What elements or tools did our entity use for creation? From what we have learned, there was nothing to create with. Thus, for the existence of all we know to happen, our entity, the Source, would be forced to use its own energy, its own power to produce—there was nothing else.

Here in the physical realm, we experience love as an emotion. NDErs tell us they were inundated with love after their physical death. But love, for the Creator, is an intricate part of its being. Together with its consciousness, love is the energy used to create. Which we see as Creative Consciousness.

This illustrates our intricate connection to the Creative Energy Force. It is difficult to imagine the Original Force not creating. The instant we think of that vast intelligence coupled with Love Power we can connect it with universal creation.

Our reality is the Source experiencing Itself.

That statement has been made in numerous ways, as far back as Taoism and Zen first came to the world; we are One life force creation.

Sadder than a Shakespearian tragedy, few of us realize the glory of our being. Such thoughts, we have been taught, are egotistical and self-centered. Yet those who educate us also do not realize their own wondrous reality.

No blame can be assigned for our lack of understanding. As though lining up for our annual shot, each generation before us received the same injection of knowledge and was inoculated with a lack of confidence and misunderstanding. Fear has become a stalking predator penetrating the world. Yet when we stop to look within, we find that still, quiet reality that is honest and eternal.

In his amazing book, *Man's Search for Meaning*,[31] Victor Frankl tells of his experiences as a prisoner in a Nazi concentration camp. That was where he came to the realization that each one of us has a deep inner part of us that is ours. It is a part of us that can never be taken from us unless we choose to give it, no matter what happens. He saw this as true freedom, the freedom of the soul within us.

Anthony de Mello tells us to "wake up and discover your true reality." He encourages us to choose a new reality of our being. He explains that we are an amazing and glorious creation of Love, and even the smallest atom of us is sacred—we are consecrated ground.

According to those who have had near-death experiences and a ream of spiritual teachers, we are already there. There is no need to strive to be closer to spirit. We already are as close as it is possible. As Yoda in *Star Wars* said, "Be—or be not; there is no try."

Dr. Norman Vincent Peale once said, "Change your thoughts, and you change your world." That's what is needed today. It is time to change our thoughts and our understanding of our reality and, in the process, change the world.[32]

Eckhart Tolle explains in his book, *The Power of Now.* "Who is this me that is responding to me? Are there two me's?" From that question posed within his thoughts, he came to find his spiritual reality. Elizabeth Kübler-Ross once said, "Death is simply a shedding of the physical body like the butterfly shedding its cocoon." And from the reports of those who have died and returned, it is easier than shedding a cocoon. That poor butterfly really must work at getting out of its cocoon. At the end of our time here on Earth, we slip from one space to another without the flap of a wing.

From the accounts above and many, many more, we are told that if we truly knew our reality, we would stand aside in awe.

Anita stresses,

If we all could only know how beautiful, resplendent, and powerful each of us are right now, right this very second, how freeing that would be to us and the world. Imagine if each of us chose to accept within us only that which contributed to the splendor of our beings. Exclusively accepting only what furthered our happiness and feeling good about ourselves. If that became our truth—as indeed, it is the only truth—it could change the world because all we know is a creation of conscious energy.

That sole understanding is the zenith point for everyone throughout the world. If each person worldwide understood the power of their core, it would bring peace and prosperity to every individual alive. It's as simple and difficult as that.

We already are all that we seek. There is nothing we need to do, it just is. We are born as wondrous creations of the universe.

We need not fret or concern ourselves by questioning if we are good enough. We already are. Like actors, who, in the end, strip off their costumes of humanity and know that they are complete and whole. Just as we were in our costume. We are not, nor were we ever broken or damaged in any way. It is only our thoughts that make it appear so. We have all the resources we need to navigate through life. Our inbuilt instincts, gut feelings, and intuitions are there to guide the way."

Debi-Sue talks about the beauty of her being and how it brought about an understanding of her reality.

When I began this, I was in a deep, black heart hurt clear to my bones. My experience freed me of that, and bliss is the only word that whispers of the feeling in me.

If I were a diamond, I would be flawless, perfectly cut and beyond beautiful. I could not be loved more by that being. Not one thing in me needed to be changed. I was perfect as I was made. I felt it think to me, "As I made you, I did you perfectly!" With joy, it loved me, as I was, completely.

That which is my true and ever-living self is perfect. I didn't have to be anything but just me. The truth lies there. Unconditional love sees only the beauty and certainty of love in each living spirit.

That huge and powerful entity was receiving joy just by my being there.

A smaller glowing golden light came from it like a sun and the love from it was just like the large Loving Being sent out. I asked what it was. It was so pretty and loving.

It answered me. "This is you." I was seeing myself from its vision, somehow. It saw me as a beautiful, perfect, shining living being, full of love and peace, filled with joy. I saw myself as it did, a being of golden light and love.

Me! I was beautiful! It didn't just tell me. It showed me. It loved me for the first time I could remember. I could have cried with the joy of seeing I was loving, just like it was.

Leonard shared with us when he talked about his life review. He had a heart attack in the hospital and, after watching the doctors and nurses work on his body, went to the light. He explains our reality in his own way.

Before creation, there was only us, united in one small point of awareness. Our consciousness had knowledge, but we couldn't experience it. We separated into billions of individual consciousnesses and created a universe to go there and have fun!

We are eternal beings! We weren't created because we have always existed, without a beginning or an end! We are Source experiencing itself through matter. Life is an unending circle of learning and growth.

The Positive Energy Force (us) is a vibration and love. It is this vibration that creates light. The more we love, the faster the vibration and the more we emit light.

When I was out of my body, I wondered what I looked like. Then I saw myself, and I was a light. I was made of light! However, strangely, at some point, even this light-body didn't really exist. In reality, I was just a point of consciousness in the universe!

Nanci shared her thoughts with us when we talked about Creation. Now, she once more brings her wisdom to our table of information.

After I entered the Light, at first all I saw nothing but Light. There were no sounds or smells, nothing. I was totally alone with my thoughts. That awareness was filled with dramatic revelations. Foremost among them was the recognition that I am not a human being. That, what I'd been calling my soul is who I really am. And that is not a human being, but conversely a separately existing spiritual being who is temporarily inhabiting a human body.

Lynn K Russell

Here is what **Rev. Juliet** tells us of our reality. Her story here is a bit different than any other report. Juliet meets with five other entities, and eventually, they merge into one. That is where we pick up her story.

But now, our merged entity of six moved forward, deeper and deeper into the Light to rejoin Source's core. As we neared it, I understood more and more about the universe and our place within it, as well as my own nature as Source. It became excruciatingly clear that our universe transpires exclusively within the mind of Source. There is only one being in our universe—Source. All things that we perceive as physical reality are really thoughts manifested of the Source within its own energy field. And, most importantly, none of it ever leaves Source. So, I intimately experienced the "knowing" that I am literally part of Source's thoughts. The illusion that I am separate from it is a gift from Source to itself in order that Source might fully explore its own personality and creativity.

Patsy was a devout Southern Baptist whose life revolved around the church and her faith. While dead, she learned a completely different actuality than what she had come to believe and her true reality. Here, she talks about going back into her body.

When I entered my body, I have never felt such joy. I was entranced with this incredible body I had created. I was aware of the consciousness of each cell in my body. I felt the joy of my blood as it rushed through my veins. Each cell sang its energy as it joined in sharing of the creation of new life. I deeply understood what the phrase "I sang the body electric" meant. I was so blown away by this wondrous creation, which I, as Source, had created. The loving cooperation between all my cells that joined together to create this marvelous body called Patsy. I, too, joined in this wonderous song of life and thanked each of them and praised them. I felt the energy as it journeyed through my nerve paths to its target. How alive and vital my body was. It was a marvelous creation. The cooperation of the cells as they joyfully worked together in perfect synchronization, exuberantly celebrating life. As long as I wear this body, I will never forget that experience in that moment.

Denise was a divorced mother with two small children and worked two jobs to keep the pieces together. Because she had no sick benefits when she became ill with the flu, she refused to take time off either job. Bit by bit, her illness became worse and worse, and Denise eventually died. It is a bit humorous because when she crossed over, she told her guide she needed to use the bathroom.

Through gesturing, I knew he wanted me to walk forward. I knew I'd see something like a mirror that would explain why I didn't need a bathroom. As I moved in the direction indicated, before me was a liquid pool of white that also appeared to be a mirror. I became totally mesmerized by colors, brilliant colors everywhere; I was before an array of beautiful, moving, shimmering, vibrating colors. He came close to me and asked me if I understood now. I recognized I was pure spiritual energy and One with a flowing consciousness while remaining "Denise."

Mary had an amazing event when she went through a death experience in the middle of a potentially deadly accident. There was a car on the highway in front of her, a semi close behind her, and she knew she was going to die. In the split second before the accident happened, she had what Dr. Long calls a fear-death experience. They occur when impending death is staring at them and contain all the same classical elements as an NDE without death actually happening. She returned with wonderful lessons a fraction of a second before the accident. A voice told her what to do to make the accident less serious and, in the end, saved several lives.

Source was by my side throughout the experience. I recognized I was making many poor choices because I wasn't trusting and appreciating myself. I spent too much time comparing myself to others and behaving how I thought I was supposed to. I was like a little mouse in a maze, trying to find my way, but getting nowhere.

I was astonished at how important we all are to the Creator and especially how important I was. I didn't think God knew I existed. I thought of all the years I had spent beating myself up. Then I was asked, "Why would I go through all the trouble to make you just the way you are if I wanted you to try and be like someone else?" No other person could do the job I came here to do in the same way I would. That's why it is so important not be judgmental one another. Some of us are here to teach, some to learn, and some to do both.

I first asked my mother what happens when we die when I was eight or nine. That was the day my quest for answers to what it's all about began. The journey has taken me from fascination to frustration and on to satisfaction in a relentless pursuit for solutions. It was the research into near-death experiences that finally brought the pieces together...well, almost. There are still questions I would love to know. I'm not there yet.

One of the most difficult areas for me was the statement that everything is as it should be. Clearly, the many major issues the world is dealing with today cannot be what they are talking about.

At very long last, I have an understanding. While I share it with you, know that this is my interpretation, and you may not agree. But, of course, that has been your prerogative throughout this book.

The statement, everything is as it should be, refers to the larger plan and does not offer support for how it is working out for our planet.

The major plan is for Source to know its own existence from a physical perspective. Souls are sent out to experience life, and it's up to us what we do with it. Like children at play, what games we choose and how is our decision.

When a soul comes to our world, it usually has complete amnesia of any other existence it may have had. The soul brings the past lessons it has gained throughout other lifetimes, whether we remember them or not.

Within the rules of existence, we have complete freewill. For Source to gain from experiencing this lifetime along with us, it is essential that we have absolute free choice. Otherwise no benefit could be offered to Source.

Throughout this book, three major lessons have been offered. The first is that we are all One soul experiencing this life. Another is that we are far more exquisite than we can ever imagine. The third lesson is that we create the world we live in through our thoughts. The way we see ourselves, others and the world dictates our decisions. No god is waving a magic wand. We cannot ask God to do things for us because we *are* that creative force. It's all the same thing. It is like asking ourselves to help ourselves.

When we don't look within for our answers, we are denying our reality. When we say things like, "Why doesn't God…we deny our reality. And any time we judge and refuse to bless others, we deny our reality.

People who have had an NDE return to tell us of the magnificent beauty of the other dimension. They talk of gardens and luxurious buildings. We understand that each person has the experience that is right for them. But this makes sense when we realize that we are the ones creating them.

Our creativity is not something we can turn on and off like the kitchen tap. We are constantly being Source and perpetually creating every second of every day.

Most of us don't seem to have difficulty knowing that we create our own death experience. Yet we have difficulty accepting that we are doing the same thing right here, right now. There is never a time when we are not manifesting our world, universe, and death experience.

Thought is our creative force. So, what does that mean to the world. We are not intentionally saying, let's have a pandemic, or let's have racism, or war, or the many other issues we see today. No, that is not how it works.

What we are doing is denying our reality. We are so brainwashed to believe that we are wrong, bad, stupid, and the list goes on. When I was working as a family counselor, I was astonished at how many people have such poor attitudes about themselves. The day we accept our magnificence is the day we will find total peace in the world.

26

Beyond NDEs

We move around the world with complete confidence that gravity will keep us firmly planted on the Earth. We trust that the world is solid enough to hold us up. We don't dispute that we can walk to our cars and get in and move around the planet in any direction without falling through. When we want to pick something up, we can do so if it doesn't weigh too much or nailed down. And yet further studies reveal this is nothing more than a magician's trick.

The behavior of particles has and is still taking scientists on a carnival ride of wild discoveries and insane consequences.

Science now reveals that matter is as illusive and as misleading as a mirage in the desert. The physical world we interact with is not real. As we have learned in the chapters above, this is also the understanding of those with NDEs. Now, science is opening the curtain and peeking out to explore this concept.

It was only when another very well-known physicist, David Bohm, suggested that the objective reality we think we live in does not actually exist that the universe appeared as one giant hologram.

Michael Talbot wrote about Dr. Bohm's observations in his book, *The Holographic Universe.* He explained that scientists realized, at the quantum level, that space does not exist in the way we understand. The universe gives the appearance that it is three-dimensional. Yet, when measured, it shows itself to be two-dimensional. Further examinations show that it actually doesn't exist at all. Einstein is quite clear about time and space being one thing and that they are illusions. No matter where scientists looked, there was only the perpetual now staring back at them.

The swirl of information gained from the quantum plane was true not only at that level; the same also held true for everything we know, including each one of us. Through tests, scientists found that the physical body—indeed, the material world is energy. Every element in the physical world, no matter what it is, has energy at its base.

This realization brought the discovery that we are made of the exact same energy found within the universe. Indeed, this is where Einstein's E=MC2 comes in because it is through the compressed merging of electromagnetic energy that every solid object has been united into the form of matter. We, too, are a part of that never-ending dance of energy and have a great deal of influence on everything.

We tend to think of the universe as out there, far away. But that is also an illusion. If we think of images we have seen of our planet out in space, we see that the universe surrounds us. But it goes further than that. The universe is right beside us. It surrounds us and is a part of the air we breathe.

At the quantum level, we are connected to everything in the universe and beyond. We are the essential means of our own consciousness.

Lynne McTaggart writes in her book, *The Field*, "They [scientists] also discovered that we were made of the same basic material. On our most fundamental level, living beings, including human beings, were packets of quantum energy constantly exchanging information with this inexhaustible energy sea." McTaggart does a marvelous job of explaining our connection to the quantum energy mentioned above. (If you are interested in learning more on this subject, I suggest you read McTaggart's books.)

The fact that we are, right this moment, having a direct effect, not only in our own lives, not only on this world but throughout the whole universe. This can be both humbling and mind-boggling. We are not simply a biological entity created through evolution; each one of us has taken an active role in the creation of the universe, galaxies, and the world we live in. We have been an intricate part of the creation of ourselves, right down to the genetics of our DNA.

Eckhart Tolle asks us to stop long enough to find that part of us that is the reality of our being. St. Francis of Assisi says, "What we search for is the one who sees." And now we know that is us.

It is a delight, then, to find quantum theory and the near-death experience agree. Both lead us to realize we are far greater than ever imagined. We are the Creator and the Source of all we know, and it is only our tiny, insignificant egos that keep us from recognizing our true glory.

I hope that we will come to see our reality through this book and the amazing messages shared within. The work of numerous other authors mentioned here may take you further on your journey. Then you will learn your reality and realize the wonder of you.

Endnotes

[1] Helen Schucman and William Thetford, A Course in Miracles, New York: Foundation for Inner Peace, 1976.

[2] Joel Goldsmith was a spiritual speaker and writer of numerous books around the 1940s and beyond. His books are published by The Infinite Way, a company he established.

[3] Stephen Jay Gould, ed., Book of Life (Viking 1993) pg. 219.

[4] Dr. Raymond Moody MD, Life After Life: The Investigation of a Phenomenon—Survival of Bodily Death; (1975, 1976 repr. San Francisco: HarperCollins 2001).

[5] Linda Stewart is now a moderator of an NDE chat site open to everyone interested in the subject; reach her site at http://groups.yahoo.com/group/nde/

[6] Dr. Elisabeth Kubler-Ross, On Death and Dying. Simon and Schuster/Collier books, 1970

[7] Long, J. (2014). Near-Death Experiences Evidence for Their Reality. Missouri Medicine, 111(5), 372-380. https://www.ncbi.nlm.nih.gov/pmc/articles/PMC6172100/

[8] Long, J. (2014). Near-Death Experiences Evidence for Their Reality. Missouri Medicine, 111(5), 372-380. https://www.ncbi.nlm.nih.gov/pmc/articles/PMC6172100/

[9] Dr. Sabom MD, the author of Recollections of Death, talks about the Atlantic Study from a fundamentalist Christian perspective.

[10] Along with Herbert Jasper, Dr. Wilder Penfield published Epilepsy and the Functional Anatomy of the Human Brain

(Oxford Journal of Medicine, Brain, Volume 77, Issue 4).

[11] Dr. Karl Jansen, MD, PhD, developed the chemical Ketamine and wrote Ketamine; Dreams and Realities (Multidisciplinary Association for Psychedelic Studies 2004).

[12] Dr. K. Ring and Sharon Cooper Mindsight (William James Center for Consciousness Studies 1999)

[13] Yogananda, a famous Hindu guru, came to America and taught his philosophy; George Harrison of the Beatles was one of his adherents. He wrote Autobiography of a Yogi, instrumental in perpetuating Eastern philosophy in the West.

[14] Rev. Juliet N. eventually left this world permanently, and her daughter has kept her website going: towardthelight.org.

[15] Thich Nhat Han is a well-known Buddhist monk from Vietnam, a writer, poet, speaker, and peace activist who now lives in France. http//:www.plumvillage.org

[16] Ken Wilber is an American author of A Brief History of Everything (Shambhala 2000) on developmental psychology and philosophy: he developed the Integral Theory.

[17] Lynne McTaggart is the author of the best-selling book The Field (HarperCollins 2001). She has since written many books on spirituality.

[18] Michael Talbot, The Holographic Universe (San Francisco HarperPerennial/HarperCollins 1991).

[19] Debi-Sue Weiler, or DW, has written a book about her amazing experience, Dead Is Just a Four Letter Word. You can read it free online at http://1way2see.com/ and listen to an interview with her.

[20] Dr. (Charles) Bruce Greyson, MD, co-authored Irreducible Minds and The Handbook of Near-Death Experiences: Thirty Years of Investigation (ABC-CLIO).

[21] Nicholas J. Postgate, Early Mesopotamia: Society and Economy at the Dawn of History (Routledge, 2004).

[22] Rt. Rev. Tom Wright, Dr. Helen Bond, Dr. Nicolas Baker-Brian, and Dr. Richard Holloway, History of the Devil, video produced by Lost Worlds.

[23] Ian Stevenson: a psychiatrist, researcher of reincarnation, and author of numerous books on the subject.

[24] Dr. Kenneth Ring: a professor at the University of Connecticut; is the co-founder and past president of the International Association for Near-Death Studies (IANDS); and is well known for research work proving the existence of the near-death experience. He is the author of several books on NDEs.

[25] Dr. Jim B. Tucker is the medical director of the Child and Family Psychiatry Clinic and associate professor of psychiatry and neurobehavioral sciences at the University of Virginia. His main research interests are children who remember previous lives and prenatal and birth memories. He is the author of Life Before Life: A Scientific Investigation of Children's Memories of Previous Lives (St. Martin's Press 2005), an overview of over forty years of reincarnation research at the Division of Perceptual Studies.

[26] Dr. Brian L. Weiss, an American psychiatrist, has researched reincarnation, past-life regression, future-life progression, and the survival of the human soul after death.

[27] Thomas Sawyer's near-death experience is extensive and an excellent read. He has written a book with Sydney Farr, What Thomas Sawyer Learned from Dying, available through Amazon.

[28] Dr. Melvin Morse, associate professor of pediatrics at the University of Washington, studied children's near-death experiences for several years and wrote several best-selling books on NDEs.

[29] Rev. Irving S. Cooper, Reincarnation, The Hope of the World: (1927: repr. San Diego) The Book Tree 2007.

[30] Michio Kaku, a professor of theoretical physics at City University in New York City, is a writer, lecturer, and science entertainer. His books include Parallel Worlds, A Journey Through Creation, Higher Dimensions, and the Future of the Cosmos (Anchor Books, 2005), and Physics of the Impossible, A Scientific Exploration into the World of Phasers, Force Fields, Teleportation, and Time Travel (Doubleday, 2008).

[31] Dr. Victor Frankl was a German Jewish doctor during World War II. While in a Nazi concentration camp, he developed Logo Therapy, a very positive philosophy. He is the author of Man's Search for Meaning (Washington Square Press, 1985).

[32] Dr. Norman Vincent Peale was an American Methodist minister who wrote The Power of Positive Thinking (Fawcett Columbine Trade Paper Edition 1996). He wrote many motivational books.